少林七十二藝練法

金警鐘

述古及今
闡於後學
現身說法
強國強魂者

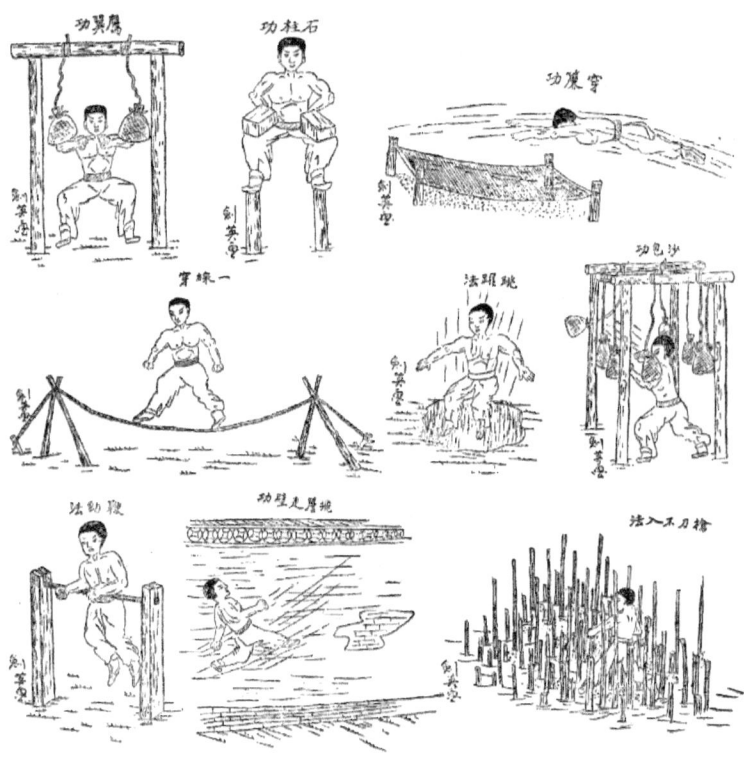

Shaolin Kung Fu Online Library

www.kungfulibrary.com

AUTHENTIC SHAOLIN HERITAGE SERIES

For the first time the book describes full training methods in all 72 Shaolin Arts. Being until recently for outsiders the most secret part of training of Shaolin monks, which made them invulnerable in fight, 72 Shaolin Arts at the present time become available to all who are ready to practice them persistently and with an open heart. Training methods described in the book allow to develop supernatural abilities, far beyond abilities of an ordinary man.

少林七十二藝練法

AUTHENTIC SHAOLIN HERITAGE

TRAINING METHODS OF 72 ARTS

OF SHAOLIN

Translated from Chinese

First edition: Tanjin, 1934

金警鐘

Jin Jing Zhong

Andrew Timofeevich (Translator)

Also by Jin Jing Zhong: *DIAN XUE SHU (DIM MAK): Skill of Acting on Acupoints.*

Editor of the translation Andrew Timofeevich. Translated by Wang Ke Ze, Leonid Serbin, Ekaterina Buga, Oleg Korshunov.

Book design by Andrew Timofeevich and Olga Akimova.

Published by Shaolin Kung Fu Online Library

USA, 2024   IS

ISBN: 979-8-9919633-9-8

shaolinkungfulibrary.com

Disclaimer:

The author and publisher of this material are not responsible in any manner whatsoever for any injury whish may occur through reading or following the instruction in this manual. The activities, physical or otherwise, described in this material may be too strenuous or dangerous for some people, and the reader should consult a physician before engaging in them.

One must not use his Power for deception of people.

One must not rise over other people.

One must not use this Art for suppression of people.

If there are achievements, there should be flaws.

It is necessary to know about flaws to attain higher achievements.

It is necessary to breed the true greatness of Spirit.

/Miao Xing/

"The Shaolin Martial Art has absorbed a lot of schools and styles. 72 Shaolin Arts are the top of true mastership."

/Shaolin Tutor Ru Jing/

"72 Shaolin Arts are perfect exercises. First of all, it is necessary to assimilate the hornbook of mastership. Apt moment, apt time, apt mystery... Strictly observe instructions, and you will be able to become as perfect as the Dragon."

/Shaolin Tutor Chun Jin/

Achievements of Monks-Warriors

Chronicles of the Shaolin Monastery (Shaolin Si Zhi) preserved for us many names of monks-warriors from Shaolin who attained mystic heights of mastery and obtained superhuman abilities thanks to indefatigable training and diligent observance of true methods. For instance, monk Hong Wen who lived in the XIII-th century sat into the stance MA, put a stone slab weighing 50 kg on his head, stood a man on each knee and stayed so until a huge incense candle, as high as a man, half burned off. His disciple Jue Yuan could dodge several spears thrown at him, broke stone slabs with his fist, knocked a hollow in a wall with his finger, ground pebbles into powder in his palms, handled all kinds of Shaolin weapons with skill.

Monk Zhi Yin who lived in the XV-th century came to Shaolin at the age of sixteen. He gained such a mastery that he could easily move a stone weighing 500 kg with a push of his leg, break trees with kick, drive piles into ground with his heel, knock down several people at once with a kick.

Monk Shu Ran who lived in the XVII-th century perfectly mastered the art of "Light Body" QING GONG, jumped out of one pit into another, could jump up a wall or a high pole, and for it he was nicknamed "Genuine Master of Gong Fu". His contemporary, monk Shu Qing mastered the art of "Diamond Finger" to perfection, with his finger he could pierce a wooden board as it were a straw mat and crush stones into sand with blows of his elbows.

The XIX-th century also knew a lot of true masters. Monk Ji Hui gained outstanding success in exercises for hardness YING GONG. He crushed huge stones with his elbow like with a diamond pestle and broke thick wooden beams with an arm blow. Besides, he was proficient in the art of "Golden Bell", blows of a big iron hammer did not hurt him at all.

Monk Hai Fa beat off arrows shot at him, was able of dodging spears pointed at him from a few sides. Besides, he mastered the method "A Leg Weighing 1000 Jins", he could crush a stone with a "trampling" blow and kill a man with the "Iron Fist".

Monk Zhen Yue ran up a sheer wall of three meters high and mastered the art of "Light Steps". His disciple Ru Bi achieved some success in "Hard Art" YING GONG and additionally he perceived the "Luohan's Art" LUOHAN GONG and could fight against several armed enemies in pitch darkness.

Many hundreds of monks gained outstanding results and brought fame to Martial Arts of Shaolin for ever. All of them attained such unusual abilities thanks to special secret practices traditionally called "72 Arts of Shaolin". They are the base and essence of the Shaolin Combat Training.

For the first time the book describes full training methods in all 72 Shaolin Arts. Being until recently for outsiders the most secret part of training of Shaolin monks, which made them invulnerable in fight, 72 Shaolin Arts at the present time become available to all who are ready to practice them persistently and with an open heart. Training methods described in the book allow to develop supernatural abilities, far beyond abilities of an ordinary man.

About the Author

"We collected all we had seen and heard, we gathered ancient manuscripts given to us by our tutors to compile the present edition."

/Jin Jing Zhong/

Jin Jing Zhong (alias En Zhong) was born in 1904, had an unofficial name of Zhe Chen and a nickname of Fendian Ke ("Mad"). Engaged in traditional styles Kung Fu from his childhood. Learnt the style Tan Tui ("Kicking Legs") from master Zhu Guan Peng, the Shaolin style Liu He ("Six Harmonies") from master Yiang De Shan, the style Xing Gong Quan ("The Fist of Subconscious Mastership") from master Yin De Kui, then was a disciple of Miao Xing, the Head of the Shaolin Monastery, who taught him the style Luohan Quan ("Arhat's Fist"), 72 Shaolin Arts and ancient Shaolin Treatises on Pugilistic Arts. Later trained military police. In 1933 founded "Society for Studies of Fighting Techniques" and was the head of "Weekly Magazine of National Arts."

About the Book

The book "Training Methods of 72 Arts of Shaolin" by Jin Jing Zhong is devoted to the most enigmatic and little-known aspect of training of Shaolin monks. The book was written in 1934 with blessing and direct participation of the Head of the Shaolin Monastery Reverend Miao Xing nicknamed "The Golden Arhat", one of the best Shaolin fighters of all times.

Training methods described in the book allow to develop supernatural abilities, far beyond abilities of an ordinary man. In the course of many centuries the methods were the base and core of Shaolin combat training, the most secret part carefully hidden from strangers. However, after a huge fire in 1928 that burnt down Shaolin and a greater part of its records the situation changed. An acute problem of preserving the Shaolin heritage for future generations arose. Most probably, it was the principle reason which made Miao Xing reveal one of the main secrets of Shaolin to the public.

The book presents full description of exercises and requirements to their execution, as well as the fundamentals of training theory of 72 Shaolin Arts.

The book has been translated from the Chinese language for the first time.

Contents

Part I
Introduction. Theoretical Fundamentals

Part II
Training Methods of 72 Arts of Shaolin

***

Author's Preface

I have no inclination to civil
branches of science, I was always
attracted by military path. In my
childhood I often played war,
attacked and took defense. When
I read some war stories, I forgot
about everything. Clothed in
black, wearing high-boots, with a
wooden sword on my back, I sat
astride on a wooden bench and
imagined that I was galloping on a
horse back toward some noble
feats. It was none other than
manifestation of my nature. My
ancestors were well-known
people, they passed their
Mastership from generation to
generation, but after the decline of
the monarchy[1] they gradually
started to depart from this
tradition. My ancestors realized
that my nature was open to the
Martial Arts, therefore they started
to teach me in acrobatics and
combat technique of Shaolin.

Editor's notes:
[1] The author means Qing dynasty (1644-1911) that ruled before Xinhai
Revolution of 1911 in China.

When I grew up, I became a disciple of tutor Zhu Guan Peng who taught me the ancient style Tan Tui ("Kicking") and the technique of dislocation of bones and joints (Yu Gu). Tutor Zhu knew this method very well.

Then I was a disciple of tutor Yang De Shan and studied the Shaolin style Liu He Quan ("Fist of Six Harmonies"). The requirements were very strict and I had to do my best. Time, five years of training, passed quickly. During those years I trained myself when it was hot and when it was cold, did not stop lessons even at days-off and during holidays. I trained myself all the same, even if I was very busy in social activities. During those

five years I managed to master four kinds of Gong Fu and gradually comprehended profound sense of the Martial Arts.

There were a lot of excellent masters, and I often thought about my further studies with the aim of deeper understanding of the Martial Arts. At that time I happened to meet tutor Yin De Kui. Then he was over 80 years old. In the past he roamed provinces of Shanxi, Shenxi, Hunan, Hubei, Sichuan, Guizhou, had

popularity and good reputation. In his time he received inheritance from tutor Zhang, his skills were superb. I instantly understood that he was an excellent master and I became his apprentice with his permission. Senior disciple Guo Ze Yi replacing the tutor taught us skills. Sometime the tutor himself helped him and gave instructions to us. As Guo Ze Yi had already learnt from the tutor during 30 years, he mastered all that was the most valuable and reached perfection. That's why to learn from him meant the same as to learn from the very tutor. Our tutor was very good at "instinctive" Gong Fu, it is also called "supernatural" Gong Fu. This style differs from other schools, it rests upon the subconscious and uses hidden psychic forces, that's why it was called Xing Gong Quan – "The Fist of Subconscious Mastership". This Gong Fu has other names too: Ren Zu Men ("Teaching of Ancestors") and San Huan Men ("School of Three Emperors").

I, twenty years old lad, left civil service and fully devoted myself to military affairs, diligently worked as an instructor and trained myself in Kung Fu. Nevertheless, I often felt doubts. Fortunately, I met a lot of practiced people experienced in Kung Fu, a lot of like-minded persons. They helped and admonished me. I learnt many valuable things from them. In the mountains of Songshan I met His Reverend Miao Xing, the Head of the Shaolin Monastery, the living legend of that time. He liked my purposefulness and he started to teach me the style Luohan Quan, the 72 kinds of Shaolin Arts, methods of hitting acupoints and acupuncture (Dian Xue), technique of joint dislocation (Yu Gu), methods of grappling (Chin Na), and many other things.

I am grateful to my lucky star for being engaged in the Martial Arts for 21 years. I listened to admonitions of my Tutors and learnt a lot. I was born in a family of officials, but never had I a habit to enjoy respect and luxury, that's why I succeeded in getting good results. Moreover, I diligently learnt and all my tutors were well-known people. During whole my life I was engaged in the Martial Arts, I was taught, I did my best, all other pursuits were sacrificed to it. Was it done only to improve health or to become a tutor in Kung Fu and a hawker who sells a complex of movements (TAO)? Our Martial Arts are important means of strengthening the Nation and the State. Unfortunately, many Wu Shu masters put on airs and stagnated. They keep secrets from each other and don't share experience. It will be of no good. That's why we publish for the country all we have got and appeal for everybody to support our initiative and spread it. Let our Martial Art like the rising sun shines for the whole world, let our country be among powerful states. We collected all we had seen and heard, we gathered ancient manuscripts given to us by our tutors to compile the present book series. We hope that readers will make their comments that could be used to introduce corrections into the second possible editions.

Mad Jin Jing Zhong from the family of Yanjing.

Wrote it in the House of Dilapidated Books and Blunt Sword on the 1-st of March 23-th year of Chinese Republic (1934).

Certificate for passing Government examination belonging to the author.

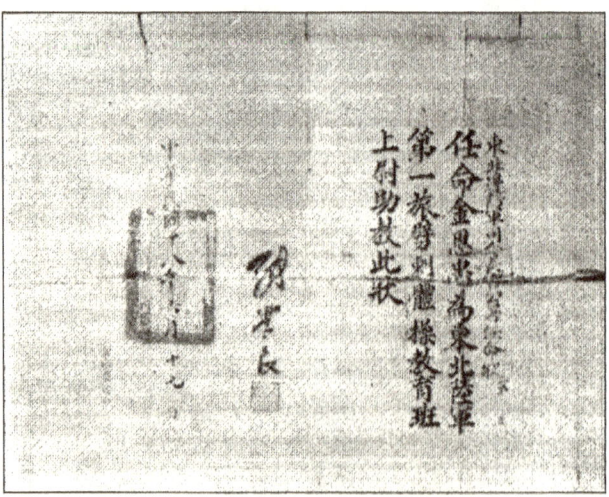

Training Certificate belonging to the author.

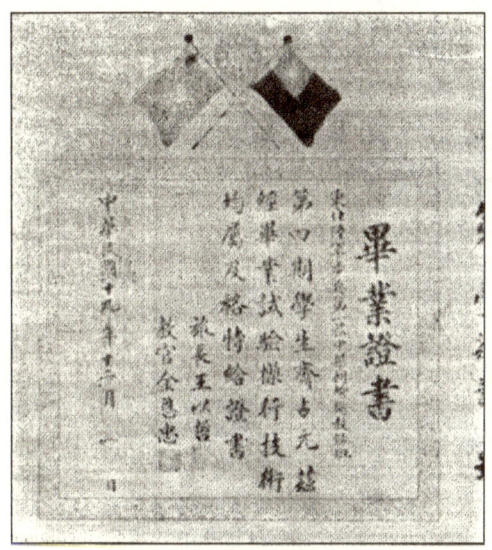

Diploma in teaching belonging to the author.

Honorary medal presented to the author.

Honorary gold medal presented to the author.

Gold medal "For Valour" presented to the author.

Bai Li Xian
(Painter)

Bai Li Xian in military uniform.

The compilers. From the right to the left: Jin Xiao Tian, Jin Jing Zhong, Jin Zhuang Fei.

Short Biographies of the Compilers

Jin En Zhong, elder brother, second name Ze Chen, nickname Mad, pen-name Jing Zhong, 30 years old, born in the noble family of Yanjing, went for his lessons to a private school of Yuying in the Chinese capital. He was taught acrobatics and Shaolin Wu Shu at home. Then became a disciple of tutor Zhu Guan Peng who taught him the style Tan Tui. Later mastered the Shaolin style Liu He Quan from tutor Yang De Shan. Also learnt "Subconscious Gong Fu" from tutor Ying De Kui. Besides, for a long time was a disciple of His Reverence Miao Xing, the Head of the Shaolin Monastery.

Served in the North-Eastern Army as company commander, deputy battalion commander, head of an auditing department, staff officer, battalion commander, senior coach in hand-to-hand combat and head of a training department. Wrote manuals for bayonet combat, theory and methods of bayonet handling, saber combat, hand-to-hand combat. He also wrote a book about famous Wu Shu masters and several other works.

Participated in all-China review of Martial Arts (Wu Shu), sports games of four North-Eastern provinces, Chinese-Japanese competitions in Martial Arts, Wu Shu exhibition competition in Tanjin. He built up the "Society for promotion of WU SHU" in the town of Shenshui. Has friendly and social character, no traits of a martinet at all. Now serves in police of the town of Jinmeng. His level of skills is quite high. He has common

muscles, at first sight he does not look like a man who is engaged in Wu Shu.

Jin En Liang, second name Jia Tian, assumed name Xiao Tian, second (middle) brother, 28 years old, finished the school of Yuying, worked as a fireman at the Police department of the capital, then served as squad commander in capital gendarmerie, inspecting officer and aide-de-camp attached to garrison headquarters. Now works in a Tanjin newspaper.

In his childhood learnt acrobatics and Shaolin Wu Shu. Then became a disciple of Yiang Jing Qing, a Taiji Quan (Tai Chi Chuan) master, learnt technique of Taiji Quan with a sword. In Tanjin together with Bai Ji Chuan and others (all of them are disciples of Tutor Sun Lu Tang) built up a society "Peng Fei" for learning Wu Shu where he spared no efforts in his work. His Gong Fu belongs to "flexible" (or "soft") type, so his muscles are not developed too much.

Jin En Shan, second name Ze Ming, assumed name Zhuang Fei, the third (junior) brother, 26 years old, took his lessons at the school of Yuying, served as squad commander in tank troops of the North-Eastern Army, sergeant-major in a reconnaissance brigade of the 34-th division, then signal platoon commander of the 1-st brigade of land forces. In his childhood learnt acrobatics and Shaolin Wu Shu, then became a disciple of tutor-wrestler Dai Lao San. Dai Lao San is also known as known in five northern provinces are Shen San and Bao San. Recently practices an exercise called "Frog" from "72 kinds of the Martial Art of Shaolin". His Gong Fu belongs to "hard" type, so his muscles are well developed.

Biography of the Reverend Miao Xing

The Reverend Miao Xing, the second name Wen Hao, nickname "Golden Arhat", was born in the town of Dengfeng, Henan province. In his childhood he indulged in WU SHU, writing and calligraphy, he especially liked the Buddhistic Teaching. When he was twenty years old, his level of mastership became quite high, but he continued to perfect himself. He started to travel regions close to the valley of Yangtze river, met many famous people. Together they discussed various problems, and those personal contacts gave Miao Xing a lot of useful things.

Later Miao Sing served in the army and rose to the rank of a regiment commander. However, he himself thought that his combat mastership had not reached a sufficient level. That's why he decided to leave the army and passed to peaceful occupations. After the retirement he returned to his native land where he was quietly engaged in agriculture, read sutras and improved his combat mastership.

In such a way several years passed. Miao Xing felt that the situation in the country was critical, the people had misfortunes, social morals were in decay. Full of shame and annoyance, he came to a Buddhistic temple in the mountains of Songshan and

took monastic vows. Monks of the Shaolin Monastery mastered combat Gong Fu to perfection, it was known to the whole country. Although lately great losses were inflicted to that cause, but fortunately, thanks to efforts of great modern masters it did not disappear. After taking of monastic vows His Reverend Miao Xing continued to be engaged in the Martial Arts for health.

Soon the Head of the Monastery paid attention to a new monk. Sizing him up, he was greatly surprised: by that time Miao Xing's mastership (Gong Fu) was next to perfection. Miao Xing was granted the highest privilege: the Head of the Monastery personally started to pass to Miao Xing the ancestral Martial Art of Shaolin and various kinds of Gong Fu, for example, "Pole for Defending Mountains", "Subconscious (Intuitive) Art of Luohan for Defending the Gate of the Temple", technique of pressing on acupoints with fingers, technique of joint dislocation, art of locks, methods of training the internal energy Qi (QI GONG) and many others. When laymen challenged (Shaolin monks), each time Miao Xing was sent to engage in a trial of strength and each time he won, gaining the highest prestige among monks. He was nominated to the position of the Temple Keeper. Besides, he was responsible for training monks and laymen.

After the death of the Head of the Monastery according to his testament Miao Xing took this post. By general decision of all monks he was also nominated to the position of the Senior

Tutor and was responsible for training, as he was a direct heir[2] of the true tradition of the Shaolin School.

Miao Xing had a lot of disciples - over five thousand monks and over two hundred laymen. I was one of his disciples. He always thought that training other people was his duty and took an oath to eliminate the tradition held in the past "not to pass secrets" in order to develop the Martial Art for consolidation of the nation and the state. So, many secrets of the Shaolin Martial Art that was not revealed before became known to laymen at Miao Xing's time. It speaks about generous nature and warm heart of the Reverend. Besides, he wrote many books, in particular, "The Genealogical Tree and Source of the Shaolin School", "Explanation of the Shaolin Pugilistic Art (Shaolin Quan)", "Explanations of the Shaolin Staff", "Sutra (Canon) of Five Da Mo Styles", "Diagram of Chan Zhang (Dhyana)", "Interpretation of the Shaolin Precepts", "A Few More Precious Words about Fist and Weapon" and some others. Those books were carefully kept in our temple; unfortunately, they were not published. In 1928 I, being a member of a military delegation, visited Shaolin and my tutor gave me hand-written copies of books "Luohan Quan", "Methods of Using the Sword of Bai

---

Editor's notes:

[2] Each Shaolin monk belongs to a certain generation (SHI). As a legend says, the first generation was represented by Bodhidharma (DA MO) himself, but the actual count starts from the Head of the Monastery Fu Yu who lived in the XIII-th century. A disciple of a monk belongs to a generation which follows the tutor's generation. If they said that Miao Xing was "a direct heir of the true tradition of the Shaolin school", it meant that his tutor was the Head of the Monastery himself and his "genealogy" was on the main trunk of multi-branched genealogical tree of Shaolin monks.

Yuan", "72 Kinds of Martial Art" and "Secrets of Intuitive Gong Fu". Guided by directions of the Tutor, I compiled books which were published at different times.

I never forgot precepts of my Tutor. Recently I wrote to my tutor a letter and asked him to send his photo. Only then I knew that as soon as last year my Tutor reached Nirvana. He was only 58 years old... When I knew about it, I could not suppress my tears. My Tutor was not only in command of the Martial Art, his Humanities were also amazing. Being a highly educated man, he made a valuable contribution into the preservation and the development of the Shaolin School and his services were very great. This book was compiled on the base of manuscripts presented to me by him. I hope that it will meet expectations of the readers. In conclusion I attach mournful saying in honor of my Tutor.

Dedicated to His Reverend Miao Xing

Oh majestic Golden Arhat,
Thou art in command of any weapon,
Of the sword Jian, the Spear and the sword of Dao.
Thou art also skilful in a pugilistic struggle,
Thou art like a soaring Dragon
And a Tiger ready to jump.
Thou hast the martial Spirit,
Thou art of extraordinary valor.

- 33 -

Oh, brave, courageous monk,
Thy endurance exceeds that one of stone and iron,
Thy will is incomparably hard.
Thou developed the national culture,
Saved our nation.
Thy heart is wide-opened,
Thy Spirit is ever-victorious!

Discourse of the Tutor Miao Xing about Training Exercises (LIAN GONG) and Training of Combat Technique (DI GONG)

One must not use his Strength for deception of people.
One must not rise over other people.
One must not use this Art for suppression of people.

If there are achievements, there should be flaws.
It is necessary to know about flaws to attain higher achievements.

It is necessary to breed the true greatness of Spirit.

Quoth the tutor Miao Xing: "For that one who embarked on the study of a combat technique, Virtue (DE) that does not bend down before force is of great importance, makes much of defense and does not rely on aggression. Virtue is present in the heart and in feelings. If there is an effort, thoughts are in disarray. Therefore, defense is birth, attack is death.

If an enemy attacks, peace reigns in my soul, my breath is concentrated, I am courageous and brave. When thoughts and breath are in peace and steadiness, only then QI[3], flourishing and powerful, is born. If an enemy attacks, there should be no place for worry. The enemy, full of fury, attacks; if "six souls" fly into a rage, then no readiness in defense is available, it means spirit becomes weaker and QI dissipates. The enemy is strong and I lose coolness of spirit. That's why if some fracas occurs somewhere, one should be calm and imperturbable. If there is no great need to kill, you retreat in a jiffy.

Therefore, a man who trains mastership (GONG FU), at the same time trains combat knacks. It is necessary to realize it well and success will come. The Pugilistic Arts and the Weapon Handling Arts are like fire, GONG FU and its usage gives a stable ground for shaping a man. But if you are not able to apply mastership, it means the core has petrified and in decline. The people of old generations said so: "If you make fire and do not move aside, you burn yourself; to study only fighting technique without end means self-destruction". I, an old monk, say so: it makes no difference if you train GONG FU or study Fighting: first of all, you need to breed QI.

Editor's notes:

[3] QI, or CHI – internal energy of a man.

If QI is seething, Spirit SHEN is filled; if the Spirit is vigorous, the strength is enough; if strength is enough, the whole body is strong and sound, muscles and bones are strong and sturdy, the soul and natural talents become magic. When you attain it, it is no need for you to attack, honor or dishonor means nothing, the might of the Martial Art can not be thrown down, wind and rain, the cold and the heat are harmless. Anything harmful (to an ordinary man) can not already do a harm when you attain this state. It is of no importance if you train GONG FU (exercises) or fighting skills – everything is aimed at this, it is only necessary to avoid uneasiness (fuss).

What does it mean – to breed QI? They say, if you understand that life and death are only false illusions, you can tell the truth from a lie and a variety of things will be kept in your heart; then deep meditation will break your bondage to emotions and aspirations. It is necessary to root out pernicious habits, especially beware of violent wrath. If everything goes in proper way, you train mastership (GONG FU) of Seventy-two Arts, improve your health and body.

However, it needs resolution and determination – this is the most important! It is necessary to give yourself to this cause every day, one must not do it at one's fancy, at one's own will. It is also necessary to deeply understand the essence of the Buddhist teaching, keep in breast "grief and sorrow", introduce purity and elegance into GONG FU, it should not be just preparation for a fight to defend yourself. Equally, one should be aware of life's lures and

should not be a slave of his desires. If you bravely engage in a mortal combat, I, an old monk, say on this occasion: it is also necessary to dispel apprehensions and fears of novices, rear courage and finally, in using GONG FU, to counteract its petrifaction.

I insistently warn you: be cautious! Contemporaries, training both internal mastery (GONG FU) and fighting technique, must improve their nature according to those directions, try to do the best, be modest and remain in shadow, avoid such a situation when "one burns oneself while making fire"; don't do any harm (to other people). It is necessary to strive for a true result in training GONG FU and fighting technique with all one's might, then you fortify your body and make your life longer. All these will yield a well-deserved and excellent result!

Quoth Lao Tse: "If man's thoughts are pure, but he feels worry in his heart, he needs peace in his heart. Emotions and desires paralyze, it is necessary to avoid emotions with all one's might, then the heart will find peace and become limpid in natural way, the Spirit will purify itself in natural course. Then "Six natural emotions" can not produce "Three banes, or poisons[4]." This dictum from the practice of Taoism Teaching is quite difficult for understanding. I,

---

Editor's notes:

[4] Three "banes", or "poisons" in Buddhism are three negative qualities: 1) greediness and sexual desires; 2) fury and ill will; 3) folly and delusions.

an old monk, who practices both internal exercises (GONG FU) and fighting technique, would like to say: if you can understand it, Peace will rein in your heart and Purity in your soul. Then even in a brutal and bloody fight you can free yourself (from bondage of emotions), fortify your body, that is the main purport of self-preservation.

In a sense, the man seeking achievements through training in GONG FU and fighting technique paves the path resembling the path of "Contemplation" (i.e. meditation in Chan Buddhism). But alongside with resemblance, there are some differences. Especially great difference is that (in the first case) the body is fortified, resources of self-defense increase, the trinity JING[5], QI and SHEN breed, which is the best Art of self-preservation. If only one component of the trinity is poor, it affects the other elements. As the saying goes, "if one leaf falls down, autumn comes to the Celestial Empire[6]".

It is possible to give birth to QI through JING, QI can give birth to SHEN, nourishing vital forces form an entity, everything should follow the established order. At first – "breeding vitality", then – fighting. At first it is necessary to breed JING and when JING replenishes, QI can be strengthened, when QI is strong, Spirit SHEN boils with

---

Editor's notes:

[5] JIN - "Fundamental principle" of a human being, fundamentals and source of life and development.
[6] "Celestial Empire" - an old name for China or the Chinese Empire.

energy, if SHEN is energetic, the body is healthy, if the body is healthy, diseases have no chance to penetrate.

From generation to generation GONG FU and fighting technique are trained according to the above-said and it is a very important thing. It is necessary to perceive the purport of exercises, overcome movement with immobility, replace turbidity with purity, not to show the people (your skill), not to cause prejudice, face all external misfortunes, difficulties and offences indifferently and cheerfully. One should not take mockeries of miserable liars very much to heart, their insults and jeers do not come to heart. Spirit SHEN concentrates and strives for unity to guard its truth, in this case "six emotions" can not come into existence and dwell in you, "three banes" can not be born, the Spirit will be Pure and the heart will be in Peace. Then your GONG FU will be able to reach the highest mastership VISHAYA[7]. Truth is comprehended in combination of achievements in "breeding vitality" and the fighting art."

Editor's notes:

[7] VISHAYA - Buddhistic notion of "the utmost".

Part I:
Introduction.
Theoretical
Fundamentals

"I insistently warn you: be cautious! Contemporaries, training both internal mastery (GONG FU) and fighting technique, must improve their nature according to those directions, try to do the best, be modest and remain in shadow, avoid such a situation when "one burns oneself while making fire"; don't do any harm (to other people). It is necessary to strive for a true result in training GONG FU and fighting technique with all one's might, then you fortify your body and make your life longer. All these will yield a well-deserved and excellent result!"

/Miao Xing/

1.1 72 Kinds of Shaolin Martial Art in combination with Pugilistic techniques and Weapon

When you train the Martial Art (WU SHU), besides learning pugilistic and weapon handling techniques you have to pay serious attention to so called "soft" and "hard" Gong Fu. You use pugilistic and weapon handling techniques in a combat and Gong Fu is the basis of pugilistic technique and weapon handling. Therefore, great masters master not only the combat technique in perfection, but also gain great results in Gong Fu.

Fiction and poetry about ancient heroes often mentioned that so-and-so mastered "Palm of Iron Shot" (TIE SHA ZHANG) and so-and-so mastered "Covering oneself with the Golden Bell" (JIN ZHONG ZHAO). Thanks to that skill they defeated the enemy. As to its gist, Gong Fu are subdivided into four kinds: soft, hard, internal and external Gong Fu. The soft Gong Fu corresponds with YIN and the hard Gong Fu YANG[8] is used to deliver blows. The internal Gong Fu trains the internal energy QI and the external Gong Fu trains the force LI.

Editor's notes:

[8] YANG and YIN – two forces or principles in Chinese philosophy: YANG - bright, active, masculine, spiritual force or principle in the universe; YIN – dark, passive, feminine, material force or principle in the universe.

It is more difficult to train oneself in the soft Gong Fu. By his appearance a man in command of the soft Gong Fu looks like an ordinary man, but if he is punched or struck with some weapon, the blow enters him as if it is cotton wool and the man receives no damages. But if it is he who punches even from a distance of a few CHI[9] without touching an enemy, the enemy will fall dawn all the same. This effect of the soft Gong Fu astonishes (the uninitiated); indeed, softness gains the upper hand over hardness! That is YIN of the soft Gong Fu.

It is easier to perfect oneself in the hard Gong Fu. A well-trained man, having concentrated the force Li and the energy QI at a proper place, is able to bear sword blows. Or he lies on a board with nails, their sharp ends up, after it a stone slab of several hundreds JINs[10] is laid upon him and the slab is struck with a sledge-hammer. The slab will be broken, but no harm will be done to the man. It astonishes the people. The hard Gong Fu personifies the masculine force YANG. A lot of people train themselves in the hard Gong Fu, but the progress made is different. Soft, hard, internal and external Gong Fu have a lot of different kinds, their number is not limited by seventy-two. Moreover, each kind includes two or three exercises. Here, in this book, we shall consider only 72 kinds of Gong Fu. For example, "Cinnabar Palm" (ZHU SHA ZHANG), "An Hand of the Sun Rays" (YANG GUANG SHOU) and others belong to

---

Editor's notes:

[9] CHI is a unit of length equal to about 30 cm.
[10] JIN is a unit of weight equal to 0.5 kg.

the soft Gong Fu. "Covering oneself with the Golden Bell" (JIN ZHONG ZHAO), "Iron Shirt" (TIE BU SHAN GONG) and others belong to the hard Gong Fu. The exercise "Frog" (HAMA GONG) and others are the internal Gong Fu. "Iron Bull" (TIE NIU GONG), "Sluice Shutter weighing 1000 JINs" (QIAN JIN ZHA) and others are the external Gong Fu.

When you gain some success (in training), you will have a good health, swords and spears can not wound you, no disease can penetrate your body, you will not fear wind and rain, cold or heat. Moreover, if you are in command of pugilistic combat techniques and weapon, you will honorably extricate yourself from any difficulties. So, Gong Fu must be blended with the pugilistic art and weapon handling technique, they should not be separated. In a combination each component fully reveals its possibilities, but being separated, it loses its efficiency. Masters of the Martial Arts say: "If you practise pugilistic technique and do not train Gong Fu, you will not achieve anything till your old age".

1.2 Effect of 72 Shaolin Arts on Breath QI and Blood XUE

YIN and YANG are present in all four Gong Fu, softness and hardness, in all 72 kinds of Martial Arts the internal force (QI) and blood (XUE) are determining factors. QI acts as defense and XUE as nourishment. All people have "nourishment" and "defense". So they say that "nourishment" is impossible without "defense", but equally "defense" is impossible without "nourishment". However, QI is the prevailing element and XUE is secondary one. In other words, "defense" holds the first place and "nourishment" the second, because if XUE is not sufficient, one can produce it, but a man instantly dies without QI. That's why QI determines life and death of a man.

QI comes into existence in ZHONG JIAO[11] and concentrates in the region of lungs. QI moves on the surface of the entire body and inside of it, day and night without stopping for an instant. QI is also motive power of blood circulation. XUE, blood, is the quintessence of water and cereals diluted in the spleen and the stomach. Blood concentrates in the heart and from there is supplied to the kidneys and the lung from a signal

---

Editor's notes:

[11] ZHONG JIAO - upper part of the stomach, solar plexus.

- 45 -

sent by the liver. Blood circulates throughout the whole body, it includes red and white components. The eyes, having received blood, can see. The ears, having received blood, can hear. The hands, having received blood, can take. The feet, having received blood, can walk. It means one should accumulate QI and feed the body with blood XUE.

Generally speaking, QI and XUE supplement each other, that's why at no account one should harm them. When QI and XUE join together, the internal organs work well. Then appetite is good, YANG and YIN breed. Main channels where vital force, blood and nutrients circulate will be full. If feelings are muddled, will has disappeared, QI is weak, XUE is insufficient, the mood is cheerless, the clean seems to be the dirty, movement is obstructed. QI outside is lost, XUE inside flows with hindrance, therefore all sorts diseases appear, a danger of death arises.

A man with full XUE looks healthy, but if he has weak QI, he grows decrepit. It is very difficult to properly cultivate QI and XUE and it is very easy to harm them. Therefore, one should be extremely careful. The way for the preservation of QI and replenishment of XUE lies through training in combat technique and Gong Fu. To practise Gong Fu means to train QI. During training time QI sets into motion XUE and it circulates throughout the entire body. In such a way, step by step, you become strong and firm. You will be protected against epidemics of dangerous diseases, you will not be afraid of cold and heat, you will get out of any mess with confidence and overcome any difficulties. But for it you must strain every effort. QI should be trained to such a level that it could concentrate in

any part of your body by an order of your will – from axillary ribs to finger tips. At the same time breathing volume (the volume of the chest) increases, appetite becomes better. From day to day your health, mind and will are improved. A well-trained man has a good health and strong will, therefore he can control his destiny.

As a matter of fact, a strong or a weak man is the same as strong or weak QI or XUE. The life and death of a man is the same as the life and death of QI and XUE. The development of a man is the same as the development of QI and XUE. Isn't the correlation between them very strong?

1.3 72 Kinds of Shaolin Martial Art and Man's Internal Organs

When executing exercises from 72 Arts, the main point is peace of mind and concentration. It is necessary to give up extraneous thoughts, not allow an outside evil (distracting factors) intrude (into your mind), and shun inner (thoughts). The method of treatment of internal organs consists in harmonizing them. Then the sick will cure his disease and the healthy will make his body and nervous system stronger. The heart should be pure, it is necessary to foster high moral qualities, it is necessary to form clearness of purpose. If after that you engage in GONG FU, you will get excellent results.

The method of treatment of internal organs consists in the following: each day before the ZI WU hours[12], it is necessary to sit in a comfortable posture, chatter the teeth and swallow your spittle. Then, it is necessary to read the rule of six hieroglyphs: HE, XU, HU, SI, CHUI and XI. It is possible to cure diseases of internal organs in such a way. The rule says: pronounce hieroglyph XU for the liver with the open eyes. Pronounce hieroglyph SI for the lungs with the arms raised up. Pronounce

---

Editor's notes:

[12] "ZI WU hours" is noon and midnight.

hieroglyph HE for the heart with the arms joined above the head. Pronounce hieroglyph CHUI for the kidney with the arms around your knees. Pronounce hieroglyph HU for the spleen with the lips protruded to the front and rounded. Pronounce hieroglyph XI for "Three Heaters"[13]. That is the method of treatment of internal organs. Internal organs is the residence of QI and JING. If they are not sound, how can one get good results in GONG FU? That's why it is necessary to pronounce six sounds each day before training - to eliminate inner evil and prevent outside evil from penetration. It is necessary to concentrate attention, fill (the body) with QI, then strength will be in abundance and only then you can quickly get a good result.

Recitative said by the time of conducting exercises according hieroglyphs:

• *The young XU clears the eyes, the tree supports the liver; in summer days the fire in the heart becomes quiet with the help of HE.*

• *HE and SI establish and collect metal, water the lungs; in winter CHUI of water comes to life in proper GONG AN[14].*

Editor's notes:

[13] "Three Heaters" (SAN JIAO) in Chinese traditional medicine is a conventional organ that combines the functions of several organs. The upper heater summarizes the functions of the heart and the lungs in the distribution of QI and blood for nourishment of different organs and tissues. The middle heater summarizes the functions of the spleen and the stomach in digestion and absorption of nutrients. The lower heater summarizes the functions of the kidneys and bladder, controls water exchange and secretions.
[14] GONG AN, lit. "the Palace of Tranquillity".

• In "Three Heaters" ZHANG GONG[15] eliminates heat with the help of XI, during four seasons HU in the spleen digests food.

One should beware of sound being heard with the ears[16]. This exercise is really able to protect the Spirit and Cinnabar Pill (DAN TIAN).

Shaolin tutor Chun Nian says:

"Six hieroglyphs is the key to "rearing life", prolongation of life and elimination of many diseases. Train yourself every day at a certain time without any breaks, after all, it is an excellent method of preserving health."

Editor's notes:

[15] ZHANG GONG, lit. "Chief of a Palace".
[16] It is meant that those hieroglyphs are pronounced in low voice, almost unheard, during a long outward breath.

1.4 72 Shaolin Arts and Age

Everybody can train himself in 72 kinds of the Shaolin Gong Fu. Everybody has QI, therefore, he has physical strength too. If you have physical strength, you can train yourself. However, your age should be taken into consideration. Children are naive and spontaneous; they do not worry about anything except food and sleep. It is pure YANG. Thy are ill very seldom, they are full of vigor, they learn easier than elderly people. When they grow up, six internal desires and seven external feelings appear; as time passes, the internal organs change under the pressure of internal and external evils and at that time it is difficult to train oneself. If a man is able to reject bad thoughts, forget about lust, calm himself, concentrate his attention and efforts, he can also attain success. Therefore, people in WU SHU circles give lessons for children from one to six years old to train their arms and legs and do massage of their muscles, then teach them to handle various kinds of small arms. It is called Gong Fu for children. Internal organs of elderly people grow old; it is necessary to preserve Spirit, reject seven feelings and six desires, not worry, have good food, avoid long exposure to the cold in winter to heat in summer, do easy exercises on the regular basis, and at no account make abrupt movements. All those things promote long life.

1.5 The Difficult and the Easy in Mastering 72 Shaolin Arts

It is comparatively difficult to train oneself in 72 Arts. One should make a gradual progress step by step for a long time. Ten years fly by as one day as you go on training. Usually, it is unbearable for people. Beginners who have no appreciable effects in several months or half a year stop halfway. Others are already close to success, but being full of vanity, they also stop training. There are people with strong will who persistently train oneself and gain success. If immoral people are trained by specialists with poor professional skills, it is difficult for them to get a good result. And there are virtuous people of high moral standards who strictly follow all instructions of their tutors, they are modest and friendly, loved by all tutors, but they have little strength and poor health and can not bear a great amount of training. For them, it is also difficult to gain the aim and, therefore, achieve success and become a master.

On the other hand, it is a simple and easy thing to engage in Gong Fu. For example, such methods of the external Hard Gong Fu as "Piercing Through Stones" (DIAN SHI), "Twin Lock" (SHUANG SUO GONG), "Kicking at Wooden Pole" (TI MU ZHUANG) and others, as well as methods of the internal Soft Gong Fu: "Soft Bones" (ROU GU GONG), "Breathing in Yin" (XI YIN GONG) and others do not require special equipment. Therefore, it is possible to train oneself

anywhere and in any conditions. For instance, in the period of Ming dynasty Yuan Cheng, a well-known monk, trained blows with an open palm, using any free minute. He did it since morning till night, when he wandered about or stayed at the Shaolin Monastery, and never stopped training. Each day he perfected that blow at least 10,000 times. When he was 40 years old, he wandered in mountains in the province of Guizhou. Suddenly a tiger sprang at him. But Yuan Cheng only moved his palm and the tiger was thrown far off. One more example: at the end of the Qing dynasty Ma Xi Gong, a disciple a well-known monk, Chun Mi trained his finger all days long by poking it into a stone. When he walked or sat, he poked his finger into ground, walls, trees and other objects. In a word, he poked everywhere. Once, he sold a horse and was on his way home. On a mountain path he met a gang of robbers who wanted to rob him. Without saying a word he picked up a stone, poked into it with his finger: the stone was crushed into small pieces. The robbers ran away in fear.

So, it is simple and at the same time difficult to master the methods, because tremendous efforts are to be made for that. The main things are persistence and perseverance. That's the way to success!

1.6 Laws and Rules of 72 Arts

The aims of training in 72 Shaolin Arts are to improve health, be strong and sturdy, withstand external forces, eliminate inner diseases, protect oneself against attacks. Training should be treated seriously, don't be in hurry. Success should be gradually achieved. When exercising, one must observe Five Demands: first, be serious; second, be conscientious; third, the Spirit should conform the Will; fourth, take care of one's honor; fifth, strictly follow the methods.

There are Ten Bans for those who train oneself: laziness, conceit, haste, excessiveness, weakness for strong drinks, folly, slander, hypocrisy, lack of respect for teachers and oppression of the young. There are also Ten Harms: sexual desires that harm soul, violent rage that harms QI, excessive thoughtfulness that harms nerves, sorrow that harms heart, wine that harms blood, laziness that harms sinews, hurry that harms bones, smoking that harms lung, spicy food that harms stomach, excessive drinking that harms spleen.

If you know "Five Demands", "Ten Bans" and "Ten Harms", you can proceed to training. The training process has several stages. At first, muscles and then sinews are trained. After it one accumulates strength and then cultivates QI. If you strictly follow the methods, you will see results regardless what kind of WU SHU you practise. If you seriously treat "Five Demands" and "Ten Bans" and remember "Ten Harms", you will attain complete success and your skills will be perfect.

1.7 Training Methods of 72 Arts of Shaolin

72 Shaolin Arts are divided into "Hard" and "Soft", "Internal" and "External" and some other categories. Different kinds of Gong Fu have different training methods. The gist of Gong Fu can be comprehended with mind, it can not be expressed in words. One should clearly realize in the process of learning: if a man wishes to attain those skills to dominate the people, in time he will inevitably fall into bad habits and laziness. In that case one can not acquire the technique. Even if you have achieved something, you will come to a bad end.

It is impossible to perfect oneself in all 72 arts at the same time, but if you display persistence and perseverance, overcome all difficulties, you will gain complete success. Reverend Ji Qin, WU SHU master from the Shaolin Monastery, said: "72 Soft and Hard kinds of Gong Fu are suitable for elderly people, grown-ups and children. Children can engage in the Soft Gong Fu and middle-aged and young people can engage in QI GONG and the Hard Gong Fu. Elderly people can develop tenacity and make their life longer. The High Mountains represent training methods in complete, the main thing in all kinds is to be patient and adamant." Master, Reverend Zhen Jun said: "72 Arts are the true Gong Fu. It is necessary to train oneself during 10 years. After mastering Gong Fu you should not resort to it without good reasons. It is an unjust to use these skills for offending people. Follow the principles everywhere, obey tutors and inspiration will come."

1.8 Base Exercises which Form the Ground for Improvement in 72 Arts of Shaolin

1.8.1 Suspending a Gold Coin (XIUAN JIN QIAN)

The main purport of the exercise "Suspending a Gold Coin" is intensification of hearing and vision to develop protective reactions in case of a sudden attack of the enemy. An old copper coin with a hole can be used in the exercise: hang it on a string to a beam at the brow level. Stand close to the coin and push it to swing from your eyes. When the coin returns and reaches your eyelid, try not to wink. After attaining this you can train GONG FU with the coin being behind your back and you hearing the sound of its movement. After training for a long time the skill will spontaneously reveal itself: if you suddenly come upon a complicated situation in an encounter, you will instinctively act in accordance with circumstances and if there is unsurpassed coordination (of eyes and arms), you can not help but win.

1.8.2 Hanging Pearl of Buddha (GUA FO ZHOU)

Take two Buddhist pearls, string them and hang in the front and the back of the spot where a sitting meditation takes place at the height of brow level. Swing the pearls to the left and to the right

when meditative exercises are over: one pearl passes before your eyes, the second one behind your head. Don't wink and try to hear the sound and feel the movement behind your back at the same time, fling your arm and catch a pearl with two fingers. It is the evidence of mastership. If you are engaged and the enemy uses a secret (small) weapon[17], you can at once catch him with your hand. This is an excellent protective skill. It is possible to create a perfect man with complete reliance on the capabilities of ears and eyes.

Opinion of Shaolin monk Chun Mi:

"Eyes and ears serve the man like a scout on a horse: the eyes observe, the ears hear and (one can) be the first to react (to deliver a blow before the enemy did). If you are engaged in a deadly fight where hundreds positions follow each other, fully rely on your eyes and ears, this is the very first rule."

Editor's notes:

[17] AN QI – "dark", or "secret" weapon; traditionally Shaolin monks learn combat technique with some improvised means, in particular, with small objects which employment can be concealed from the enemy; it may be a chop stick, needle, fishing hook, small fan, coin with sharpened edge, brass-knuckles, short darting arrows etc.

1.8.3 1000 Layers of Paper (QIAN CHENG ZHI)

The purport of the exercise "One Thousand Layers of Paper" is to train blows of the hard force YIANG JING. It is a very simple exercise. Take a pile of paper containing over 1000 sheets and nail it to a wooden block. Hence, another name of this exercise is "Striking at the Paper Block"(DA ZHI DUN). Put it at the level of the waist and deliver blows with fists, palms, fingers, and elbows. Deliver blows in the immobile stance MA BU ("Rider") at first, then train yourself in movement and with jumps. Deliver "slashing" (PI) blows and "cracking" (ZA) blows while turning the torso. Deliver "slapping" blows (PAI DA) in the stance GONG BU ("Bow"). While standing sideways, deliver elbow blows: reverse and direct blows, blows from the left and from the right. Blows can be alternated and follow in a certain succession. Employ various arm techniques and imagine a combat with an enemy. If you are training in such a way for half a year, you can finish the first stage, the second stage of acquirement of the skill will be over after one year, and a complete success will be after two years of training. Punches will be rapid like rain drops during wind blasts. If a blow is delivered at the enemy whose weight is not great, he can be toppled over to the ground, if a blow is delivered at a heavy enemy, his muscles and bones can be damaged, but it is impossible to kill him. People meet difficulties in understanding the so called hard force of YANG, but one should not stop training, it is necessary to train this exercise again and again, in that case the effect will be wonderful and quick. Famous fighters could not help but train this exercise.

1.8.4 Circle RU YI (RU YI QUAN)

The exercise "Circle RU YI" is designed for the development of abilities of fingers to grip. Two metal rings like those ones with which small children play, but of small diameter allowing to clasp them with five fingers, are used. At the first stage the weight of each ring must be 3-4 JINs (1.5 to 2 kg), clasp them with fingers and make turns. After long training force is increased. One may do the exercise holding the ring with three fingers – thumb, forefinger, and the middle finger. Then, take away the middle finger and hold it with two fingers and continue to make revolutions. With this one may consider the first stage to be over. Increase the weight to 8 JINs (4 kg). Do the exercise, holding with two fingers as before and the matter will be a full success at the end. Increase the weight to 15 JINs (7.5 kg) and in that case fingers will turn into steel hooks, if you grip muscles or joints of the enemy, you can inflict painful injuries on him. For those who practise the martial art this exercise serves as the base of GONG FU. Shaolin WU SENGs[18] often train this method too and improve their combat abilities by means of this exercise. In such a way, for instance, practised monk Zi An in time of the Yuan dynasty (1279 – 1368), monks Jue Xun, Ben Lai, Beng Zheng in time of the Ming dynasty (1368 – 1644), many other GAO SENGs[19] acquired this exercise with perfection.

Editor's notes:

[18] WU SENG – lit. "monk-fighter".
[19] GAO SENG - a monk of high rank.

Shaolin WU SENG, tutor Chun Mi said:

"The iron circle RU YI is the most convenient, if you travel a great deal, you can take it with you. In your spare time, when you have nothing to do, you can train this exercise and at the crucial moment it will help you to escape danger."

1.8.5 Striking at Cotton-Wool Ball (XUAN MIAN CHUI)

It is also one of the exercises for training arms and eyes and it is not difficult too. Take a small piece of cotton-wool, roll up a ball, hang it on a thread between beams. Deliver precise blows with one or two fingers, palm, fist. One may also use spear, sword or stick for training precise blows. It is not easy for a trainee to hit the target at the first stage. However, after long training, it is possible to learn how to do perfectly so that each blow hit the target. At that stage GONG FU reaches its perfection. In a combat engagement a blow delivered can not help but hit the target. Famous fighters train this exercise for a long time. You may hang one or two balls, on the left and on the right, deliver blows in movement as if in an actual combat. When you do this exercise with perfection, it will be of no great importance on which side the enemy is, as you will be able to attack in any direction.

Opinion of Shaolin monk Ru Qing on precise blows:

"Skill in techniques is trained during several stages, they are: "Paper Block", "Iron Circle", and "Cotton-Wool Ball". If you adhere to constancy, train you for many years, you will show your mastership and employ it against the enemy at the crucial moment."

1.8.6 Striking at Wooden Dummy (DA MU REN)

This exercise is a base of the Shaolin GONG FU, and in no case it must be ignored. Take a thick log for your training and dig it into the ground 3.5 CHIs[20] deep, the height from the ground level should be 5–5.5 CHIs or, what is better, 6 CHIs. Put a beam 1.5 CHIs long in the center crosswise. It will look like a man with stretched arms: the breast and stomach in the center, the head on the top, the beam is like two arms, one leg below. Wrap it around with cotton-wool and leather outside. A trainee stands before the dummy and employs clasps, pressing, pushing or strokes with fingers at points on the upper part of the dummy. He sets against the dummy with his buttocks and hips and pushes to its middle part. He kicks with his feet at the lower part. Imagining different parts of the body (of the enemy), employ different arms/legs/elbows/hips/knees/feet techniques; capabilities of the whole body must be used in techniques. This exercise can be daily trained early in the morning. It is of no importance which pugilistic style you learn: training with this exercise will be of invaluable benefit!

Shaolin GAO SENG Zhen Xu said:

"Hitting a wooden dummy is a method for training of energy and force, it is necessary to exercise indefatigably and diligently since sunset till sunrise. The exercise helps to collect force into a whole single; wind, snowfall, thunder, and lightning equally take their turn[21]."

Editor's notes:

[20] CHI, a measure of length, equal to 33.3 cm.
[21] Most probably, it means that the seasons take their turn, but lessons go on.

1.8.7 Kicking at Wooden Pole (TI MU ZHUANG)

This exercise trains legs and feet. Dig a log into the ground and train in evenings such a leg work as "side kick" (CE TI), "heel forward blow" (DEN TI), "cutting blow" (TAN TI), "raking blow" (CHAN TI), "inward blow" (KOU TI), "swinging blow" (BAI TI), and "wrapping blow" (CHAN TI)[22]. Deliver hard blows with legs, stand still, at the first stage you should not move (shift), deliver blows with both legs in turn. Later blows can be made in movement: after making a step or jumping you kick with the other leg, also change legs. Jump aside and deliver a blow. Turn and deliver a blow. Just imagine that the pole is your enemy and employ various techniques against him. For example, attack the enemy with your leg and immediately dodge, attack and defense supersede each other, employ various techniques of torso dodging, change quickly leg techniques and deliver blows at the pole. If you can break a thick pole by kicking, it shows the emergence of GONG FU. If you are engaged in a combat, you will be able to inflict a severe injury on the enemy or topple him over on the ground.

Editor's notes:

[22] All above names in this text have no descriptions, therefore an averaged translation is made on the base of the modern style CHANG QUAN.

1.8.8 Kicking at Flying Meteor (TI CHENG CHUI)

Hang on a beam three or four CHENG CHUI[23] (or cobblestones) with a size a bit bigger than a goose egg. Kick at CHENG CHUIs to swing them to different sides. If each blow hits the aim, one can say that the first stage has ended with success. If you deliver blows at four objects, each time hitting the aim, and CHENG CHUIs swing without touching the body, your kicks can be regarded as masterful ones and you will be capable of controlling the situation by means of kicking. This exercise trains the precision of kicking at aims, one must train oneself to exclude missing. It is the hard force of YANG by its nature. You improve force along with training your eyes.

Opinion of Shaolin tutor Ji Jing:

"In exercises "Kicking at a Wooden Pole", "Kicking at a Flying Meteor" you train force and leg work. If you manifest unbending will in continuous process of perfection, you will beat the enemy again and again, your movements must be steady."

Editor's notes:

[23] CHENG CHUI – one of the kinds of flexible weapon LIU XING CHUI, lit. "hammer-meteor", it is an iron or stone ball on a long cord.

1.9 Essentials of "Internal" and "External" Skills in 72 Shaolin Arts

1.9.1 Twenty requirements to be observed when doing "internal" and "external" exercises.

It is necessary to massage face often, rub eyes often, tug at ears, clench teeth, warm up (keep in warm) back, protect breast, massage stomach, rub feet, swallow saliva, limber up waist, feel knees, rotate elbows, keep shoulders straightly, rotate wrists and ankles, control YIN (to restrain sexual desires), thump ribs and back, butt with head, pay attention to pelvic bones, feel (press) thighs.

1.9.2 Sixteen prohibitions in training the "internal" and the "external".

Avoid of bumping your head (lit., "kowtow", the act of kneeling and touching the ground with the forehead to show great reverence) if you rose early in the morning, avoid of shady desires, avarice and disappointments, avoid of sitting on wet grass for a long time, avoid of being exposed to the cold in clothes wet from sweat, avoid of wearing thick clothes in very hot weather, avoid of fanning yourself when you sweat, avoid of burning a candle when you sleep, avoid of a sexual intercourse at the ZI time (between 11.00 p.m. and 1 a.m.), avoid of pouring cold water over your muscles, avoid of burning your skin with

hot water, avoid of drinking cold drinks after a sexual intercourse, avoid of training when your are drunk (or have a hang-over), avoid of training actively (lit. "greedily") when you don't feel well, avoid of hardness, rage, hastiness, avoid of heat, avoid of the dissipation of vigor and spirit, avoid of stopping half-way.

1.9.3 Twenty harms to be avoided when training the "internal" and the "external".

Looking for a long time is harmful JING[24], listening for a long time is harmful to the spirit SHEN[25], lying for a long time is harmful to QI, sitting for a long time is harmful to vascular system (MAI), standing for a long time is harmful to bones, walking for a long time is harmful to muscles, wild rage is harmful to liver, thoughts are harmful to spleen, very deep sorrow is harmful to vascular system; excessive gluttony is harmful to stomach, unwarranted fear is harmful to kidneys; joy in abundance is harmful to spleen, talking too much is harmful to the liquid, excessive spitting is harmful to saliva, abundant sweat is harmful to YANG , weeping too much is harmful to blood, a lot of social contacts (excessive sociability) are harmful to marrow, great chagrin is harmful to heart, long sadness is harmful to brain, overworking is harmful to strength.

Editor's notes:

[24] JING, "reproducing energy", the basis of the vital force of the man; in Taoist alchemy JING transforms into QI and QI into the spiritual energy SHEN.
[25] SHEN, spiritual energy, spirituality, spirit.

1.10 Exercises for head, face, ears, nose, eyes, and mouth as a base for improvements in 72 Shaolin Arts

1.10.1 Exercise for the head (SHOU GONG)

Both hands cover both ear orifices, tug at ears with the second finger, make ringing in the ears with the palm, it is possible to get rid of harmful QI, wind and water. Twist your neck with both hands, casting a glance on the right and on the left, shoulders and arms follow the turn, both hands clasp the head and rub it.

1.10.2 Exercise for the face (MIAN GONG)

At first, rub both palms together to reach extreme heat, then rub your face with them. The whole face should be rubbed well as if you wipe off sweat. Then, after spitting at your hands, rub your face again. Both hands massage the face with effort from inside outward, gradually descending and gliding over the face, it should be done 9 times altogether, then massage your forehead 9 times.

1.10.3 Exercise for the ears (ER GONG)

Both hands press on ER LON and rub upward and downward. Take a seat straightly, straighten one leg and draw in the other, raise both arms to the horizontal level, both palms are vertical and directed forward as if they push a door. Twisting your neck, cast a glance back on the left and on the right, 7 times altogether to each side. Put both forefingers to ear passages, turn outside 9 times. This exercise is called "clever ear" (CONG ER GONG).

1.10.4 Exercises for the eyes (MU GONG)

Each time, after waking up, rub your eyes with back sides of your thumbs 14 times without opening the eyes. Keeping eyelids tightly closed as before, roll your eyes round in a circle, 7 times to each sense of rotation. Without widely opening your eyes, massage both points CUAN ZHU 36 times with joints after bending both thumbs. Then rub your palms, both eyes look up, and massage points ER GEN 36 times with hands. Both hands rub your forehead anti-clockwise, massage from the center of brows 36 times, swallow saliva as before. Squat so that both arms are set against the ground, turn your head with force and look back to the left, then back to the right, do so 7 times. That is so called "tiger's look" (HU SHI). Rub outward your eyes with the beginning of thumbs on their external side 36 times. Move the middle fingers down from eye corners on the side of the bridge of the nose 36 times. It is also called "method of clear eyes" (MING MU FA).

1.10.5 Exercises for the nose (BI GONG)

Rub the back sides of the thumbs to reach heat, rub both sides of the nose with them 36 times. Then, rub the points YING XIANG from above downward with the forefingers 36 times.

1.10.6 Exercise for the mouth (KOU GONG)

Each time, doing the exercise for the mouth, it should be kept tightly closed. If you feel hot and dry in the mouth, bitter taste and no saliva, or there is an inflammation in the throat so that it is impossible to take food, in that case you get a fever and you have to keep the mouth widely open. Breathe out with a sound HE over 10 times, "beat the Celestial Drum" 9 times, stir saliva in your mouth, repeat outward breath HE and swallow (saliva) again. After appearing clean fluid in the mouth the heat syndrome may be eliminated. That exercise is called "beating the celestial drum" (MING TIEN GU). Your tong props up the palate and massage it, it causes the secretion of saliva and you will not feel thirsty. If there are no dryness and pathological changes in the mouth, you can advance in GONG FU, strengthen your body and bones, extend your lifetime.

1.11 Exercises for tongue, teeth, and body

1.11.1 Exercise for the tongue (SHE GONG)

The tongue props up the palate, which causes saliva secretion, saliva should be rinsed in the mouth and swallowed. Swallowing saliva in great amount promotes digestion; you may increase nourishment to strengthen your organism and if the organism is strong, the training process will wonderfully speed up.

1.11.2 Exercises for the teeth (CHI GONG)

By clenching teeth 36 times, it is possible to accumulate "the initial spirit" (YANSHEN). It is necessary tightly clench teeth when urinating. "The initial spirit" accumulates, (the body) is suffused with strength and energy, the spirit radiates fullness, one can strengthen one's health and extend one's lifetime.

1.11.3 Exercises for the body (SHEN GONG)

Sit, bending knees; a heel of one feet sets with its lower part against the beginning of the scrotum, thus preventing from "bleeding" of the substances JING and QI. The other foot should be put in such a way as to be convenient, the foot should not set against the scrotum, but at the same time it must not be suspended. After finishing to do the exercise, it is necessary to stand up slowly, one should not do abrupt arms and feet movement. It is necessary to sit straightly, keep the torso and the spine vertically, one must not tilt aside. It is necessary to spread the chest while walking and keep the head high, one must not stoop and lower the head. When lying, the torso should be kept straight, one must not bend the neck and crook the head.

1.12 Foundations of the "Internal" and "External" Skills

Everybody who goes in for GONG FU, both "soft" and "hard", must make the Spirit stronger and intensify JING, calm the Heart, accumulate QI, arrange and eliminate (distracting) thoughts and hidden fears; in doing so according the methods, you will be able to score success.

Below is explained how to prepare oneself for training. In case you suffer from some diseases you should recover and fortify (the body) on the base of the methods given (see above). In case you have no any diseases, your internal organs are healthy, QI overflows, the body is filled with energy, it is easier to master the exercises and score results relatively quickly. If internal diseases are not cured, outer diseases intrude easily, though you will train even every day without interruption, you will not able to succeed, nothing to say about the possibility of other injuries. Therefore, those who train only jumps or sitting exercises will easily become idiots, and those who train only "spitting" or "swallowing" will get a lung disease. Those who do not exercise "internal" and "external" work (simultaneously, well-balanced) will not get a good result. An outer harmful intrusion will manifest itself in a graver inner disease, that will lead to a lot of severe ailments and no drugs will help to cure them. Therefore, earlier "16 dangers" and "20 harms" were described as well as very important methods to cure the internal organs and fortify

the body. When the internal organs become healthy, you start to train "Four-Part Exercise" from "72 Arts"; you are sure to attain the target, adding part by part in succession. Take care that when you are doing "Four-Part exercise", do it in succession, step by step, not stopping half way. The best of all is to train yourself each day, during hours of ZI and WU. During the hour of ZI (at noon), the YANG force spring up, during the hour of WU (at midnight), YIN energy spring up. It allows to join the YANG and YIN energy together. In case you train yourself only once a day, it is better to conduct training at 6:30 a.m. when YIN and YANG energy are pacified and you can increase QI. If you do not observe those rules of time, if you train yourself at your fancy, it will bring no use. The place for training must be clean and quiet, without distracting factors. If the place is very noisy or in disorder, it distracts hearing and vision and if the Spirit (SHEN) is not protected, QI is sure to dissipate. If the Spirit is in disorder and QI is dissipated, it is impossible to get a result. Furthermore, the foundation in all four parts is softness, one must not train oneself with heavy heart, forcing oneself in order to get quick results, one must not ignore "16 dangers" and "20 harms", otherwise the body can be harmed. A trainee in GONG FU must be attentive. Before training GONG FU, irrespective of doing the "internal" or the "external" exercises, you must spend 100 days to train the "Four-Part exercise". It is the foundation for training other kinds of GONG FU, it is of great use when training for a long time.

Part II:
Training Methods
of 72 Arts of
Shaolin

"72 Shaolin Arts are perfect exercises. First of all, it is necessary to assimilate the "hornbook" of mastership. Apt moment, apt time, apt mystery... Strictly observe instructions, and you will be able to become as perfect as the Dragon."

/Shaolin tutor Chun Jin/

"72 Shaolin Arts should be trained diligently, without interruption for a rest neither in winter, nor in spring, summer, and autumn. You can become a hardened man by training yourself each day over hundred times, by adhering to constancy."

/Shaolin tutor Chun Nian/

1. Method "Diamond Finger" (YI ZHI JIN GANG FA)

The method "Diamond Finger" is a "hard" exercise that strengthens the external components[26]. It belongs to the "hard" force of YANG. When the exercise attains its aim, it is possible to knock a hole in the chest with a finger and injure internal organs. When mastering this exercise, one should train his finger daily on a wall or a tree trunk, other objects can be also used. It is necessary to strike with your forefinger at a  wall or other objects, starting with a slight blow and increasing gradually its force. Don't interrupt and don't stop your training. It is the first stage on the path to mastership. The skin tears off, muscles and sinews swell and hurt, but it is necessary to continue training for a long time without any hesitation and doubts. The soft skin becomes hard. After three years of

---

Editor's notes:

[26] Strengthening of such external parameters as skin, muscles and bones is meant.

training the finger will become like a tree brunch. If you strike at some object with your finger, a visible finger print is left on it. A blow at a wood can make a hollow in it, a blow at a stone can break it, a blow at a humane body can inflict a serious wound. Train this exercise diligently for three years, concentrate efforts only on one matter and your skill will become perfect if you have inflexible will. Indeed, there are outstanding men who make every effort. Beware of mistakes and wounds and move to the planned aim. One can also train the forefinger of the left hand. Don't stop at the midway in this exercise! This GONG FU is also called "Buddha's finger". There are even verses that can be read when doing this exercise. But regularity in training is a must.

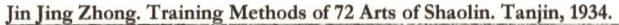

2. Exercise "Twin Lock" (SHUANG SUO GONG)

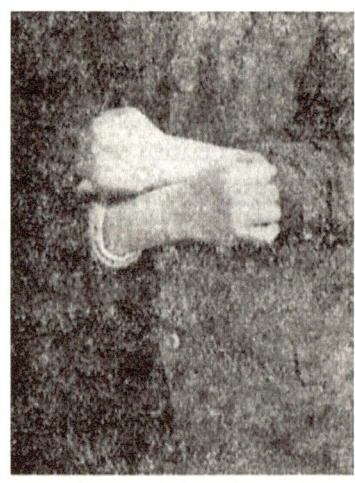

The exercise "Twin Lock" is hard in character, it strengthens muscles, bones and sinews of forearms due to external force. It is a training of the YANG hard force. Having perfected this exercise, one can withstand with bare arms an enemy armed with silent weapons. Both arms collide like straw cutters. The exercise is very simple, both forearms are trained by mutual knocks. At the first stage, one can be injured and it would be difficult to bear pain, but after training for a long time muscles become strong and the result will be excellent. Then, you will not feel pain and when striking, a thump will be heard. With this the first stage of GONGFU is over. Then wrists and fists, both palms, two fingers and single straightened finger (forefinger) are trained: in such a way mutual blows are delivered. And when a hollow thump is heard, one may stop training. With this the second stage of GONG FU, one may say, is successfully finished. Then, it is necessary to strike at feet and shin with the help of both forearms, raising the left and right knee in turn. When the skin swells, stop training. This method greatly improves the skill, because the soft is converted into the hard. In a fight with an armed enemy one can beat off his blow

with one's forearms or hands, snatch his weapon. By knocking both arms against each other and thus strengthening both forearms, hands and fingers one can break an enemy's arm and that is an excellent self-defense. But at least, you should spend three years to train this exercise. This method strengthens muscles and bones, improves blood circulation.

3. Exercise "Striking with Foot" (ZU SHE GONG)

The exercise "Striking with Foot" is a hard external exercise, it trains the hard force of YANG. It is a rather simple exercise: it is necessary to strike at small stones and other objects with a toe during morning and evening strolls. At the first stage the toes will hurt and swell, it is necessary to train it persistently for a long time, then muscles will strengthen and there will be a positive result. It is necessary to increase the force of blows gradually, do it according the principle "from the simple to the complicated", gradually proceed to striking at bigger stones. If you can throw a big stone to some distance, that is the end of the first stage on the way to mastership. One should continue training by striking aiming blows at stony objects. At that stage the skill is at the highest point. If you engage in a combat with an enemy, you will be able to throw him as far as a stone. It is necessary to approach him and deliver a blow at the lower part (of his body). Everybody, even if he firmly stands on his feet, will be flung away.

4. Exercise "Pulling out Nails" (BO DING GONG)

The exercise "Pulling out Nails" belongs to hard external training, it is the hard YANG force. It is one of the exercises which develop skill of hands, the locking force of thumb, forefinger and middle finger. The exercise is very simple. It is necessary to take a thick unabi, or jujube[27] board, knock 108 nails with length of about 3 CUNs (10 cm) into it and pull them out with the thumb and forefinger. If you can pull out nails with your hand, that is the end of the first stage on the way to mastership. Then, drive nails into a wooden board, sprinkle them with water, wait when

---

Editor's notes:

[27] Unabi, Jujube - a small tree, bearing date-like fruit and growing in China.

the nails become rusty and pull them out as it was described above. If you are able to pull out nails with your hand, your skill has reached the highest point. It is a difficult exercise at the first stage, the skin bursts, blisters bleed, that's why it is necessary to wash hands with warm solution of lake salt[28] with other ingredients after you finish doing the exercise. One may pull out 1000 nails at the last stage. In a fight you can make locks with three fingers for vulnerable spots (according to acupoints and channels) and heavily injure your enemy.

Editor's notes:

[28] "The salt from the lake of QINGHAI" in the Chinese original.

5. Exercise "Ringing Round a Tree" (BAO SHU GONG)

The exercise "Ringing Round a Tree" is also called "Maitreya" (Buddha of the future) - MILIE GONG. It is a hard external exercise belonging to the YANG force, but at the same time it trains flows of the inner force and, therefore, belongs to internal training (NEI GONG)[29]. That exercise is easily done, force of arms during a lock is trained, chest and stomach muscles are also trained. Selecting a tree which you can ring round with arms, stand before the tree, ring the trunk round with both arms tightly, squeeze it with force and try to pull the tree out. Do it several times every day and each time when you exhaust all forces, stop doing the exercise. Train yourself in such a way during one year and the strength of arms will be gradually increasing. It is necessary to gradually shake loose the trunk. If you gradually shake loose the trunk, the leaves will begin to fall off the tree. That is the end of the first stage on the way to mastership. Continue training without interruption one more year, the tree gradually withers and chest and stomach strength increases, chest and stomach muscles becomes as hard as a stone. That is the end of the second stage on the way to mastership. During the third year of training, it is necessary to continue training intensively, without stopping, in that case you

---

Editor's notes:

[29] **NEI GONG, lit. "internal work", exercises aimed at strengthening internal organs and the inner force.**

- 81 -

will have force to uproot that tree. This is full success in the exercise; after it is possible to lift a weight of 250-350 kg, rounding it with both arms. If you, being in dangerous situation, clasp your enemy with both arms, you can easily inflict a heavy injury to him. There is such a saying among specialists in martial arts: "If you practise the Martial Art during your spare time, you will be able to defend your life in a dangerous situation. The highest technique will come to your subconscious and you will be able to defeat hundreds of enemies". Indeed, it is absolutely unreasonable not to believe those words. If there are doubts left, choose a small tree - peach-tree or jujube and simply train yourself during one hundred days without aspiration for obtaining certain results. Undoubtedly, you will get an excellent result.

6. Four-Part Exercise (SI DUAN GONG)

The Four-Part exercise is a base one both in the soft and hard GONG FU of 72 Kinds of the Shaolin Martial Art. It has much in common with a known method of health improvement "Eight Pieces of Brocade" worked out by marshal Yue Fei[30] during the rule of the dynasty of SUN. Before studying the very combat technique (WU SHU) one should train the Rider's stance (MA BU) and step (movement) technique. The training stirs up interest in a man and he oftener trains himself. Then, it will not be long before the result appears. Those exercises do not need much space. Although the method is simple, its meaning is deep. We give full description of the Four-Part exercise. Successive and regular training leads to good health and long life.

Editor's notes:

[30] Yue Fei (1103-1142), national hero of China, passed all the way from a soldier to a commander of an army (marshal); is considered as the creator of two combat styles – "Eagle's Talon" and "XIN YI QUAN" along with the form BA DUAN JIN ("Eight Pieces of Brocade") which was designed for improvement of physical training of soldiers.

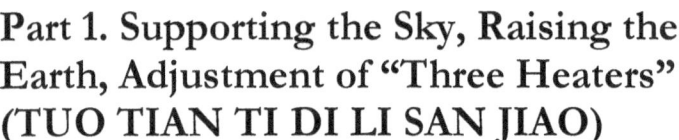

Part 1. Supporting the Sky, Raising the Earth, Adjustment of "Three Heaters" (TUO TIAN TI DI LI SAN JIAO)

Stand straight, stick out the breast, draw in your buttocks, look ahead as if you suppress a fit of anger. Fingers of both hands are closed, arms and legs are straight, knees are closed, heels and toes are joined and touch each other. Both arm are slowly moved aside from the body, do not bend the elbows, the arms are raised up as if you ring round a ball (i.e. the hands make a circle in a vertical plane), the fingers are interlocked above the head, the palms face up as if you hold a weight of 1000 JIN (500 kg). You raise your arms up with all force, look at the back of the hands, the head moves back at that, the neck strains, the jaws are clenched. Then the upper part of the body slowly tilts forward until a palm touches the floor. The lower is tilting the better. At that the legs remain to be straight, the slightest bending (in knees) is not allowed. After it the upper part of the body straightens and raises up, the arms are lowered with force, making a circle again and you take the initial position. This exercise should be done slowly.

Part 2. Five Damages, Seven Harms, Looking Back (WU LAO QI SHAN WANG HOU QIAO)

Stand straight, turn the head to the right slowly, look backward and try to see the heel of the left foot. When turning the head,

the breast sticks out, the torso is motionless, the shoulders are not tilted. Then the head turns forward to the initial position. After it the head slowly turns to the left; look backward and try to see the heel of the right foot. And again the head turns forward to the initial position. This exercise should be also done slowly.

Part 3. Opening the Window to Admire the Moon, Drive away Fire from the Heart (TUI CHUAN WANG YUE QU XIN HUO)

Set feet apart, take the Rider's stance (MA BU), the breast is put forward a little. The hands are clenched into fists and pressed to the waist with the palms up, look forward. The left leg makes a downward push and straightens, the hooked left hand as if picks up to the left, the right hand makes a push to the right with force, the torso also moves (turns) to the right. At the same time the right leg, remaining bent in knee, makes a step to the right. The eyes are fixed upon the right palm. As if you open a window and admire the moon. Then the right foot presses down and straightens (i.e. you push off with the right foot). The hooked right hand makes a semi-circle to the right. The left hand makes a push to the left with force. The body also moves (turns) to the left. Look at the left palm. In the movement the left leg makes a step to the left. Return to the initial position.

Editor's note: With a palm push the torso turns to 90 degrees and the stance "Bow and Arrows" (GONG BU) is taken: when pushing with the right palm, it is the right stance (the right bent leg is in front, the left straight leg is behind), when pushing with the left palm, it is the left stance (the left bent leg is in front, the right straight leg is behind). The push is carried out with a palm at

the breast level with the fingers pointed up and the center of the palm pointed forward. At that time the other arm is in a lower position, it is straightened in elbow and moved a little back, the hand is hooked, finger tips are gathered into a pinch and pointed upward. A palm push should use force of the torso and legs.

Part 4. Catching Emptiness, Striking at Emptiness, the Strength will not Give out (ZHAO KONG DA KONG LI BU LAO)

Set the feet aside, take the Rider's stance (MA BU). The hands are clenched into fists and pressed to the waist. Deliver a strong punch with your right fist, the fist is at shoulders level with the palm faced down. The left fist remains at its place (at the waist). The right hand opens and immediately clenches into fist again as if you catch something and at once returns to the initial position (to the waist) with force. At the same time the left arm delivers a forward blow with fist, the palm (in the process of striking) turns downward. Then the right fist strikes forward and the left hand makes a catch at that and returns back in the form of fist. Continue in such a way until your legs are tired and strength goes out, then return the left leg to the initial position. That is "Catching Emptiness, Striking at Emptiness" (ZHAO KONG DA KONG).

Although the exercise "Four parts" is short, but it is necessary to train it with a pure and quiet heart, concentrate force and attention, breathing should be freely. One must not "force" (control) breathing, one must not "conceal" (hold) breathing either. If you "force" (control) breathing excessively, breath and QI deplete and holding breath undermines QI. It is necessary to do a deep exhalation when tilting down. When you support the sky with your arms, the fingers of both hands should be interlocked, then QI will come to finger tips. It is better, if you can raise your heel a little (i.e. stand on tiptoe). When the palms touch the floor, it is necessary to avoid excessive application of force, otherwise the kidney may be injured. Don't stop halfway, don't be afraid of making progress. All movements should be done slowly with a certain force. You do not achieve success in haste, don't strive for a quick result. In the course of training you will not only improve your health and spirit but also lay a solid base for further improvement in GONG FU.

7. Exercise "One Finger of Chan Meditation" (YI ZHI CHAN GONG)

YI ZHI CHAN in 72 Shaolin Martial Arts belongs to the category YIN. It is one of the most deadly methods among the soft kinds of GONG FU. The gist of mastership is in one finger. XI HEI ZI, a well-known master of the Southern Shaolin school, is in full command of this kind of GONG FU. He studied the Martial Arts during 40 years, visited all southern and northern provinces and no man was able to overcome him.

At the very beginning when he started training, he hung a weight at the place where he often passed along at day-time. Each time, when he passed it, he poked his finger to it. He did it each time from day to day. At the beginning, when he poked his finger to the weight, it remained motionless. Then, being struck, it started to swing. After it he increased the distance between him and the weight and his finger did not touch the weight when hitting. He struck at emptiness in the direction of the weight and it started to swing. If you reach this point, you may think that you have done the first step on the way to mastering YI ZHAN CHAN.

Then he put a few lamps in the court and lighted them at night. He stood before the lamps at a distance of two ZHANGs[31] and delivered a blow with one finger. At first the flame of a lamp only swayed like it sways from a light wind. However, after some time one finger striking toward the lamp immediately extinguished the flame. It is the second stage in mastering this kind of GONG FU. After it, it is necessary to put paper shades on lamps and train oneself until striking with one finger tears paper and extinguishes flame. That is the end of the third stage. And, at last, paper shades are replaced with glass ones. When striking with one finger flame extinguishes and the glass does not get broken, it means that the aim has been attained. It needs 10 years of tenacious work. If this mastership is directed against a man, there will be no wounds seen, but the internal organs will be seriously injured. A weak blow in direction of some aqupoints can cause vascular spasm and block blood circulation. After it blood circulation can be restored only with special massage. This GONG FU is much more serious than "The Palm of Red Shot", "The Palm of Black Shot" and "Hands of Five Poisons". The only thing you need is regularity, and success will come.

Editor's notes:

[31] ZHANG is measure of length equal to 3.33 m.

8. Exercise "Iron Head" (TIE TOU GONG)

The exercise "Iron Head" is hard GONG FU, it trains external power (strength) and belongs to the category YANG. Besides, this method also has an internal aspect: it must rely on strong QI. It is necessary to train three parts of your head: top, forehead and back. Although external effect (force) is employed to strengthen skin, muscles and bones, it is also necessary to develop the internal force and QI. The head should be filled with QI and Spirit. One can achieve success if the internal and external aspect match and supplement each other. Otherwise, if only the force of external effect without supplementation of the internal force is used, you will get some result, but it will be far from perfection.

The training method is as follows: wrap several dozens of layers of a soft fabric (silk) round your head, add one or two layers of plate above and hit your head against a wall. It should be done each day, a few times a day. During training the head is being filled with QI. You should not hit with great force at first, as the top of the head is not hard yet and you can injure the brain. The head is wrapped up with fabric because of this reason. As training goes, increase the force and number of blows. It is necessary to train yourself during one year. This means that the first step has been made on the way to mastership. Take off two or three layers of fabric and continue training during 100 days. Then decrease the number of fabric layers again. To put it briefly, the greater success the smaller number of fabric layers.

At the end of the second year you may completely take off the fabric. It means that the second stage in mastering this GONG FU is over. At first, it is quite an unpleasant thing to hit the head against a wall after taking the fabric off, but in time unpleasant feelings disappear. The head will become as hard as a brick or a stone. One will be able to say that the aim has been achieved.

If this method is used against a man (as saying goes "to butt with the mutton head"), you can easily knock him down. The head of a well-trained man is harder than a stone. A head blow can split a stone slab and crumple an iron sheet. It only demands frank sincerity in training and fulfillment of all requirements with all one's heart and self-denial. It is necessary to reject all extraneous thoughts so that peace and tranquility would reign in the head. They rightly say that it is necessary to improve your character before starting to train WU SHU. In that case you will not go to deadlock and reach the destination. This kind of GONG FU is not so rare. For instance, strolling acrobats often show such exercises as "Striking with a Big Hammer at the Head" (YOU CHUI GUANG DING), "Two Dragons Dive in the Sea" (SHUANG LONG RU HAI), "Breaking Bricks" (ZA ZHUAN) and others – all this is the display of GONG FU "Iron Head". This GONG FU must be used only for self-defense, you should not be the first who delivers the blow. It is worth mentioning that it is comparatively easy to attain success in it.

9. Exercise "Iron Shirt" (TIE BU SHAN GONG)

The exercise "Iron Shirt" is hard GONG FU for the development of the external force. If you combine this exercise with training the internal power by means of TONG JIA GONG ("The art of a child", or "Children's exercises"; a complex of 16 exercises for teaching children develops flexibility, equilibrium, control of breath, steadiness, and speed), you can attain the same result as in GONG FU "Covering with Gold Bell". However, it is not easy to reach success, that's why the people in command of this GONG FU can be seldom found.

The training method of "Iron Shirt" is as follows: you should wrap round your breast, stomach and back with a few layers of soft fabric, then massage the wrapped spots with force. Bend and unbend your elbows from time to time. Don't hold your breath. It is advisable to sleep at a hard bed at night so that the body would touch a rigid surface. In due course the body becomes strong. It is somewhat difficult at first, but you will gradually get used to it. Besides, it is necessary to make a horizontal bar in the court, dig out a shallow pit under it and fill it with fine sand to a depth of 1 CHI approximately (CHI is a unit of length equal to 0.33 cm). Train yourself each day in the morning and in the evening in the following way: hang on your arms on the horizontal bar, then fall down to the pit so that some part of the body – shoulders, back, breast, stomach, buttocks etc. touch sand. During one training each part of the

body should touch sand twice in such a way. You train yourself in this way during three years.

Then you train yourself without wrapping fabric. Now you should strike at the whole body with a wooden hammer, then with an iron one. It is necessary mobilize the internal energy QI during training, concentrate attention and direct force to the spot at which you deliver a blow. It will take another three years. When the upper part of the body becomes as soft as cotton wool, it means you have mastered GONG FU "Iron Shirt". If necessary, you will be able to mobilize internal energy QI and concentrate the force Li, your body will become as hard as iron or stone. A punch or a blow with a solid object will not do you harm. But all the same, blows with a heavy weapon should be avoided.

Some of Shaolin monks are able to use this GONG FU. Once my tutor, esteemed master Wang, gave a stage performance in Peking. I was only ten years old at that time. I, moved by curiosity and forgetting about decency, took a short pike and delivered a stabbing blow at his stomach with all force. But at the same moment I was thrown off and fell flat on my back. I stood up, surprised and ravished: master Wang instantly had concentrated his internal energy QI for defense, and my attack failed.

10. Exercise "A Series of Blows" (PAI DA GONG)

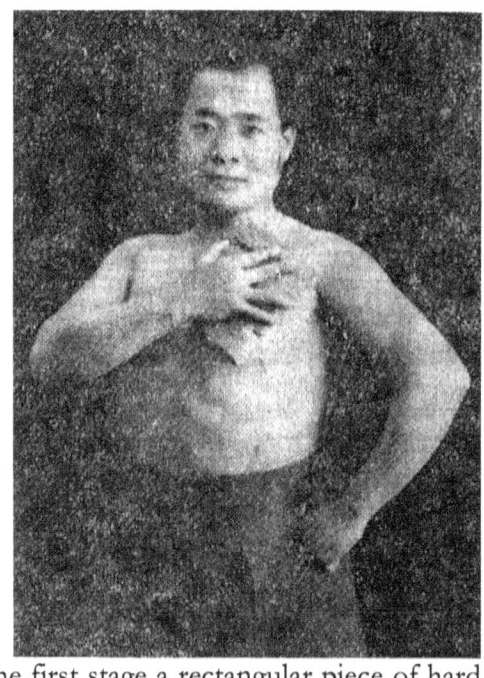

The exercise "A Series of Blows" is an external strengthening, hard exercise. Hard force is used outside, soft effort is employed inside. It is a method of hitting on the body surface to strengthen muscles and sinews, similar to the method of hitting on all parts of the body with a wooden hammer. This exercise is quite simple. What is called a series (of blows) means delivering successive blows with a brick. At the first stage a rectangular piece of hard wood, 30 cm long, 25 cm wide and 5 cm thick, is used.

You take a wooden piece in your hand and do the exercise successively by delivering blows with its side surface at all parts of your body, at first at the left shoulder and forearm, then at the right shoulder and forearm. Start from light blows and proceed to heavier ones. Make a 100 blows or more. Then,

proceed to the thighs and shins, starting from the left leg and holding the brick in the right hand, and continue with hitting on the right leg, holding (the brick) in the left hand. Then proceed to the breast and the stomach, hitting from the left to the right and holding the brick in a right hand, then on the legs (on their back and side surfaces), starting from the back of the waist. Then both sides. Train yourself every day once in the morning and once in the evening in such a way, each time hitting on different parts of the body one hundred times or more with a wooden brick. Change a wooden brick with a common baked brick after one-year training and continue training as above. Start to use "gold" brick (a brick not of gold, but of iron)[32] after another half a year. Train yourself another half a year, at this stage a certain level of mastership is reached. Continue to hit on all muscles of your body to strengthen and harden them. Of course, this method can not be compared with GONG FU "Iron Bull" (TIE NIU), thanks to it neither swords nor spears can hurt you. But if you are attacked only with fists and legs, blows will not harm you.

It is, then, necessary to strike with fists and legs at the torso, you do not inflict any injury at that. Then, continue to do the exercise and hit on different vulnerable (lit. "soft") parts of your body. It is necessary to pluck up your spirits in order not to inflict wounds or injure the internal organs. Hold your breath at the time of hitting, breathe out after a blow, then tense and deliver another blow. The head and the elbows can be trained in

---

Editor's notes:

[32] The hieroglyph "JIN" in the Chinese language means both gold and metal.

the same way. If you train yourself step by step for two years, you will be able to get a good result. This method is mostly used in five northern provinces and seldom in the South. It is employed along with the exercise "Beating a Wooden Man" (DA MU REN) at the Shaolin Monastery.

11. Exercise "Sweeping with an Iron Broom" (TIE SAO ZHOU GONG)

The exercise "Sweeping with an Iron Broom" is a hard, external strengthening exercise which belongs to YANG methods. This exercise is also called "Iron Leg" (TIE TUI GONG). It is one of exercises which develop leg skills. One or both legs can be trained. In practice a sweeping blow can be made at enemy's legs or a weapon can be knocked out from enemy's hands. This method offers great advantages in a combat. The whole force is concentrated in a leg, at that the main emphasis is made on the shin.

Executing this method of training, it is necessary to practise in standing motionless in the Rider's stance (QI MA SHI) every day. When your strength runs low, it is necessary to stop the exercise and walk to restore your strength. After rest, continue doing this exercise. There is no need to do it too long at the first stage, it is necessary to increase gradually the time of standing in the stance. If the duration is increased up to two hours and you do not feel tired, it means that the first stage of reaching mastership is over. Due to the stance "Three levels"[33] and "Five

---

Editor's notes:

[33] "Three levels" most likely mean the division of the body into three parts: upper, middle and lower part.

bodies"[34] become strong . This exercise should be done during many days and in that case the force of both legs will increase and become much greater than that one of ordinary people. When this stage is over, it is necessary to dig a wooden pole or a few poles at some distance from each other into the ground. Deliver horizontal sweeping-off blows at them without stopping. It is necessary to deliver blows with legs, using all four surfaces of a leg (front, back and side surfaces) with equal degree. The exercise can be done with one leg or with both legs simultaneously; besides, there are no certain requirements concerning the succession of blows. Perfecting the technique, you yourself can decide how to act. For instance, if you see a pole within reach, immediately make several sweeping kicks. At the first stage the muscles will pain and swell, it will be hard to train yourself, but you need to do difficult exercises for a long time and the muscle will strengthen and you will not feel pain. You will gradually shake loose poles and be able to break them at the end. Then, act according to the principle "from the simple to the complicated": take thicker poles and repeat the whole process. When the poles are broken, it is necessary to proceed to big tree.

In the beginning one should not become like a dragon-fly rocking a stone pile, one should not be after a quick result. After training during three years mastership gradually comes, kicking will give results and leaves will start to fall off the tree. Continue training, and the trunk starts to shake, it is a great success in

Editor's notes:

[34] "Five bodies", it probably means five internal organs.

obtaining mastership. Then the tree will begin to swing and it will finally fall. It is already the full success in the exercise "Sweeping with an Iron Broom". If a blow is delivered at an enemy, his bones can be broken and his muscles torn. Nobody can resist it. However, those kinds of training are difficult, one should have a strong spirit.

12. Exercise "Hand - a Bamboo Leaf" (ZHU YE SHOU GONG)

The exercise "Hand - a Bamboo Leaf"[35] is hard external exercise, also called "The Palm Rotating in Sand" (FAN SHA ZHANG). It is one the kinds of GONG FU specializing in strengthening the striking surfaces of a palm. There is some similarity with "Horse's Saddle" (MA AN GONG), the exercise for a fist, and with "Making Holes in Stones" (DIAN SHI GONG), the exercise that is aimed at strengthening and training of fingers. Those exercises make up so called "Deadly arm" (SHA SHOU).

Sew a linen bag with the surface of two square CHI[36] approximately, fill it in with iron filings, their edges should not

---

Editor's notes:

[35] The shape of a hand resembling a bamboo leaf is meant.
[36] Contemporary square CHI is equal to 0.11 square meter.

be sharp. At the initial stage the weight of the bag must be about 15 kg. A trainee ties it to a branch of a strong tree, stands on one side of the bag, takes the stance QI MA BU ("Rider") and delivers blows with his palm at the bag. As iron fillings are quite sharp, your hands can be readily injured and cut, so it is necessary to use medical tinctures to wash off hands at the first stage. Gradually, as a result of hits, dents appear in the bag. By and by the depth of dents will increase to several centimeters. When dents in fillings appear as a result of your blows, it will be necessary to hit another side of the bag. Deliver pushing blows forward with force or when (the bag) moves back (toward you), catch (the bag). If the bag, struck on its front surface, begins to rotate, do not stop the rotation and deliver a blow so that it would start rotating in opposite direction. Continue delivering blows as above. When you feel that your power is not spent during the exercise, that it is done too easily, it is necessary to increase the weight by 10 kg and continue training the exercise. Add by 10 kg in each few months to get the bag weight equal to 60 kg. When you freely deliver blows with your palms on the whole surface of the bag and you don't feel tired, it means that GONGFU has reached unsurpassed mastership. It will take about 3 or 4 years. If, after finishing your training, you strike with your hand at an object, it will break, if you strike at an enemy, you will seriously injure him. It is necessary to train both right and left hands.

13. Exercise "Jumping Centipede" (WU GONG TIAO)

The exercise "Jumping Centipede" is also called "The Art of Slithering Snake" (SHE XING SHU). It trains arm and leg skills well and spring ability at the same time.

Training method: both hands with the palms and both feet with the toes take a firm stand on the ground, holding the whole body suspended. The breast and the stomach are at a distance of 6-9 cm from the ground level. This is the starting position for the exercise. Then the lower part of the body rises a little up due to bending in the waist, at the same time both palms push off the ground with force, the toes of both feet also push off (the ground), the pushing force being directed upward and a little backward. The whole body flies up and "hangs over" in the air. Using the force of a push, it is necessary not only to jump up,

but also move forward, then land to the palms and the toes and take a firm stand on the ground; as before, the torso is at a distance of 6-9 cm from the ground level. In such a way, the initial position is assumed.

When a certain level of skill is attained in this exercise, the palms may be clenched into fists, then proceed to a support on five fingers, three fingers, two fingers and, finally, one finger (forefinger). One may also raise one foot and continue doing the exercise until it is possible to make jumps in any direction – either forward or backward. The exercise is considered to be worked through at this stage. If you encounter the enemy, the force of fingers and toes will help to overwhelm him; moreover, jumps can be used for retreat in a fight. You can press yourself close to the ground and slither like a snake if the enemy suddenly rushed to you and you could not foresee this.

14. Raising a Weight of 1000 JINs (TIE QIAN JIN)

The exercise "Raising a Weight of 1000 JINs" is a hard and external exercise that increases force. It belongs to the hard kind of force YANG. This exercise is also called "Water Chestnut" (SHI BO QI, BI QI)[37]. This kind of GONG FU trains the force of grip with thumb, middle, and forefinger (so called the force of a "pinch", or "pinching force") and increases the force of arms in a "supporting" effort. It bears certain similarity with the exercise "Eagle's Claws" (YING ZHAO) and "Pulling out a Mountain" (BO SHAN). The difference is in that in this case force is applied by the inner surfaces of the third phalanges of fingers instead of finger tips. Fighters in the South China widely used this exercise. This training can not but help to yield results even for those who have only a superficial knowledge of the Martial Art.

Hollow out of a stone a gadget (tool) resembling a vertebra, narrower in the upper part and wider in the lower part, generally resembling a fruit of the Chinese waterchestnut (i.e. of elongated, pear-like shape). The weight of the small tool can be over 10 JINs[38], and the

SHI BO QI, Chinese
waterchestnut

Editor's notes:

[37] SHI BO QI, BI QI – Chinese waterchestnut, Eleocharis tuberosa Roem. et Schult; it is so named because the shape of a training tool looks like a tuber of this plant (see the picture).
[38] Contemporary JIN is equal to 0.5 kg.

weight of the biggest tool, 60 to 70 JINs. The diameter of the base of the tool is equal to 7 to 8 CUNs[39]. The trainee holds the upper part of the tool with his three fingers, the forefinger and the middle finger are on the outer side, the thumb on the inner side, the tips of all fingers are pointed downward, to the lower part of the tool. The forefinger and the middle finger are held by the third phalanges, it is not allowable to hold the bottom of the tool with the other hand. Raise up and hold the tool hung after gripping. It is the initial stage of training. Try to raise a tool weighing 10 or more JINs vertically with three fingers and hold it as long as possible in the end. From time to time a narrow tool may be replaced with a wider one, with four even (smooth) edges on its sides so that fingers have nothing to catch. In this case it will be more difficult to fix a hold. Therefore, it is necessary to raise with a hand, but without swinging at the initial stage.

Hard training during less than a half year or one year at most, and it will be possible to easily raise and hold the tool hanging. However, it is necessary to train oneself, persistently and very much, to hold the tool for a long time. When you are exhausted, immediately put down the tool. When you become stronger, you may raise the tool and walk with it on the ground. At first, put it down after a few steps. The skill will eventually improve, the ability to hold the tool for a longer time will appear and with it a possibility to make from a few steps up to several dozens steps, and from several dozens to several hundreds steps,

---

Editor's notes:

[39] 1 CUN = 3.33 cm.

holding the tool in the hand at the same time. Then, walking on the ground in circles and holding the tool in hands, make several dozens circles. Replace the tool with a heavier one and continue training in the same way. However, do not try to increase the weight too soon, you can add about 3 JINs (1.5 kg) each time at least, but not more than 5 JINs (2.5 kg), to avoid injuries. It is necessary to advance in training gradually and step by step. You can attain the ability to hold a tool weighing 50-60 JINs (25-30 kg) with three fingers for a long time. When one succeeds in holding the tool by weight for more than one hour, the skill will reach its peak. If you catch your enemy, you will be able to inflict a severe wound on him, if you catch a wooden board with three fingers, you will be able to press a hole through it.

15. Celestial's Palm (XIAN REN ZHANG)

The exercise "Celestial's Palm" belongs to hard exercises for outer strengthening. This exercise trains to obtain so called "YANG Hand", it trains the skill of stabbing force of finger tips. There is a similar, on the face of it, exercise for a hand YIN, the soft exercise "One Finger of CHAN Meditation" (YI ZHI CHAN GONG) (see par.#7). However, those two exercises are similar only in that in both cases

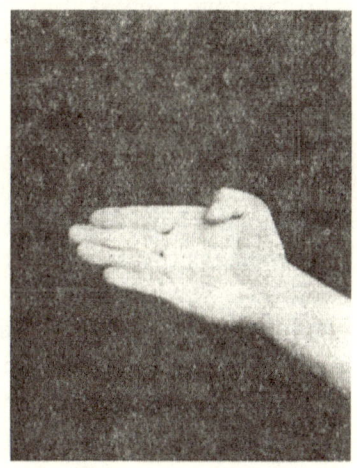

finger tips are used. Four fingers closely laid together are used in this exercise. The training method is quite simple and one can achieve a good result comparatively soon, therefore many people do it.

The method of doing the exercise: at first press together four fingers tightly, (the fingers are straight and strained) and deliver stabbing blows with force at hard objects, for instance at wall, tree, table or wooden bench. At the first stage it is not essential that it should be a definite object. Training must be carried out each day. After long training some result will be achieved, for instance, you will be able to make a small dent in a wood. The more you train, the more will be the dent, with time you will

strike a hole. Take then a big stone - a green semiprecious stone - and continue training as before. With time, after many blows, you will make a deep dent. If you deliver a blow at an enemy with this palm, you will inflict on him a severe wound. Therefore, one should be quiet and well-balanced. Even those who improve their skill in "Iron Bull" (TIE NIU GONG) and bear sword and spear blows with confidence, will not be able withstand. It is of no importance whether he knows about this technique or not: when he comes across with "Celestial's Palm", he will surely lose. A trainee in "Iron Bull" exercises hard force of YANG. Although a trainee in "Celestial's Palm" also exercises the hard force of YANG, but the soft force of YIN is also available, therefore YIN overpowers YANG. It is called "to overpower hardness with the help of softness". There is such a saying among fighters: "Training the exercise "Iron Bull", it is possible to attain perfection, but this skill becomes ineffectual against "Celestial's Palm".

When training this skill, it is better to exercise both left and right palm, in that case the enemy will not know from where a blow will be delivered. Two words (hieroglyphs) JIAN and REN – "Tenacity" and "Endurance" can be the best wishes.

16. Method of Hardness and Softness (GANG ROU FA)

Another name of "Method of Hardness and Softness" is the exercise with a paper bundle. This skill belongs to YANG category, but it also uses the vital energy QI, training in which belongs to YIN category. This GONG FU is concentrated in a fist. Although it is said to be the hard GONG FU, but you will understand in a process of training that it is not pure hardness. Actually, it is mutually complementary combination of soft and hard GONG FU.

At the first stage of training it is necessary to take a small amount of spoiled paper and tie it up with a string, shaping a bundle into a brick two CHIs (about 66 cm) long and wide, two of its opposite sides are a little longer. Tie a long cord at the butt-end to pull this weight. It is necessary to lay this paper bundle on a long table. The length of the table should be about two ZHANGs (about 6.6 m), its width should be about three CHIs (1 m). The surface of the table should consist of several boards of different width laid perpendicular to a longer side of the table. The outer boards are fixed to the frame of the table and ten odd boards at the middle are removable. A trainee stands by one of the end of the table, assumes the stance MA BU ("Rider") or GONG BU ("Bow"), takes the end of the long cord with his left hand and strikes with his right fist at the paper bundle lying near him at the end of the table. At first the bundle moves to a small distance which increases with greater skill. After a blow the left hand pulls the cord and returns the bundle

to the initial position. After one more blow return the bundle again and so on: do so until you exhaust. Then, change hands. You should train yourself each day, one time in the morning, one time in the evening. At first the weight of the paper bundle must not exceed 20 JINs (10 kg), it is comparatively easy to strike at it. Later some lead should be added to the bundle, the weight is gradually increased up to 100 JINs. If the weight is gradually increased, it is hardly noticeable for a trainee. Continue training as before: after a blow the bundle should move to some distance, the other hand returns it to the initial position. At that stage half a success is reached. The force of a punch is astonishing, but has not reached the highest degree yet. After that it is necessary to remove the narrowest board to have a chink. Strike at the bundle in the same manner and return it back. At first the bundle will fall through the chink, but after a few months it will fly over it without hindrance. It is necessary, then, to remove one more board and continue training. Gradually you will remove all the removable boards and a chink 1 ZHANG (about 3.3 m) wide will appear on the table. If, when striking, the bundle flies over the chink and then, after a jerk, comes to the initial position without falling into the chink, it means the full success.

Although a man, struck with the same force, receives an injury not as heavy as that one when GONG FU "Horse's Saddle" (MA AN GONG) is used, all the same he will fly at a distance of more than 2 ZHANGs (about 6.6 m) and fall. This method is very effective in a combat with several enemies. The gist of this method is hardness YANG, but softness YIN is also available. Thus, hardness and softness complement each other, that's why the exercise is called "Method of Hardness and Softness" (GANG ROU FA).

17. Cinnabar Palm (ZHU SHA ZHANG)

"Cinnabar Palm" is the soft GONG FU, it trains the inner power and belongs to category YIN. This exercise is also called "The Palm of Plum Blossom" (MEI HUA ZHANG) and "Palm of Red Sand" (HONG SHA ZHANG). Sometimes it is also called "Hand of Black Sand", but that is not right, because the method of "Hand of Black Sand" involves the use of special preparations to increase the inner power.

Training method: fill a tub with fine sand, immerse your hands into sand and rub them with force until you exhaust. It should be done each day in order to finally reach such level of mastership that when rubbing your hands over the vessel at a distance of one CHI (30 cm) sand in it will move in unison with hands. It means that the first stage in mastering this kind of GONG FU is over. If you strike

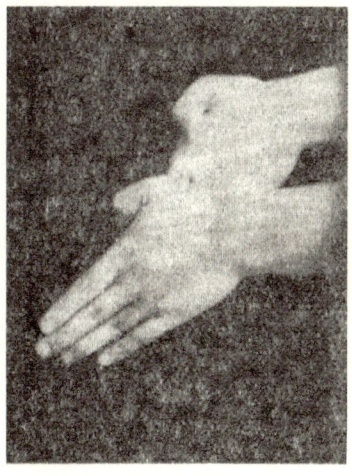

a man after that, only slightly touching his body, no outer injuries will be seen, but the inner organs will be severely, incurably wounded. While continue training, it is necessary to replace fine sand with iron shot, which later on should be replaced with iron balls weighing 4-5 LIANs[40]. If your hands do not touch the tub and the iron balls start moving after your hands, it means that the art of "Cinnabar Palm" has been mastered.

If you are in command of this GONG FU, you need not touch the enemy with hands. You make stroking movements or strike with a palm at some distance and the enemy is severely injured and will surely die in 10-15 days or even in several hours. But at least 15 years of hard work are needed to attain such skill. Being in command of this GONG FU, you must not misuse it in any case. It is a manifestation of guile and ill intentions to use it secretly. It can be used only in extremity to defend your life or the life of your near relatives. Unfounded use of this skill is immoral and disapproved by specialists in WU SHU.

Editor's notes:

[40] 1 LIAN is equal to 1/16 JIN, or 31 grams.

18. Exercise "Lying Tiger" (WO HU GONG)

The exercise "Lying Tiger" is the hard GONG FU, it trains the external power and belongs to category YANG. It is also called "GONG FU of the Sleeper" (SHUI GONG) and "Feline GONG FU" (MAO GONG). It trains the force of fingers and toes. Lie prone for training, your palms pressed to the ground are under shoulders, your elbows are bent, your legs are straight, the toes lean on the ground. Move your body forward and upward from this position. When the body is raised 1 CHI (30 cm) (above the ground), shift yourself backward and then downward. When your body is lowered to 3 CUNs (10 cm) from the ground, move forward and upward again. Repeat doing so until you are fully exhausted. From the beginning to the end of training no parts of the body but toes and palms must touch the ground. At first, after doing this exercise two or three times you will feel tired. This exercise is like press-ups made in army units. In time number of repetitions of the exercise must be gradually increased. After one year of training you will not feel tired, in that case palms must be replaced with fists. After some time fists musts be replaced with three fingers: the middle finger and forefinger in front, the thumb in back. After still more time passes you should be supported by toes of one foot with the other foot laid on it. Replace feet in turn. Then, put a stone on your back and train you with it. Increase the weight of the stone up to 100 JINs (50 kg) gradually. You will attain full success at this stage. The force of toes is not less than 1000 JINs (500 kg). Few people can endure a blow of such a force.

19. Swimming and Diving Skill (QIU SHUI SHU)

Such techniques as "Diving into Waves", "Walking on the Bottom of a Water Pool", "GONG FU of Eight Parts" are called "Swimming Skill". Earlier people called it "fitness to water environment", but today they say: "swimming technique". This skill belongs to the inner GONG FU and is based on the inner force (energy). It is in very close connection with everyday life of people. Not only those who learn WU SHU, but all the people have to learn it. For instance, you swim in a boat and suddenly the wind has risen and roughness has appeared, your boat can overturn. If you can swim, you save your life, if you can't, you can perish. The ability to swim is especially important for those who knock about the world. If a man really wants to learn swimming very well, he must train himself hard and persistently. There are some people who can swim well, but they train themselves according to European techniques. They do not know that we also have our own excellent techniques. Some pages in novels about Middle Ages knights describe how heroes show their swimming skill.

I myself know the swimming technique not too well, but I heard a lot of interesting things about it from my tutor and friends. I recorded all that and present it for your attention. In my childhood I was taught to swim by YANG, the director of the dock that was situated outside the city gates XI ZHI MENG. Once master YANG who swam very well learnt from monk CI LENG eight swimming techniques: "pushing-off", "carrying", "trampling", "swimming", "diving", "sinking", "sitting", and "jumping". Briefly speaking, the main points are as follows: a part of your body is above water, you push off with your feet; move sidewise forward as if you "carry" water on one of your shoulders; strain the vital energy QI and "trample" water; move your arms and legs and "the golden cicada glides on water faster than wind"; "dive into water and walk on the bottom"; "sink" into water with the help of arms and legs; strain QI and "sit" in water steadily; when you meet the enemy, you "jump" like a dragon. Master YANG incessantly perfected his skill. He had a nickname "tortoise" because he could be under water up to twenty minutes, moreover, he mastered the technique of water circulation through the nose.

When I just started to learn swimming, tutor YANG took me on his arms, reached a deep spot and threw me into water. I took a sip in my fright and cried: "Help me!" At that crucial moment tutor YANG caught my arm with a smile. We went out to the bank to have a rest. I recovered from fright a little and tutor YANG told me: "Next time, when you enter water, don't be afraid and don't get lost. The tutor is near you and he will help you at any moment. If you move your arms and legs in natural manner, you will not drown". As far as my temper is concerned, I am a little bit reckless, so I became much braver after those words. After entering water, I did as the tutor had told me. Although my body was not quite obedient, but water did not already cover my head. In that manner I trained myself under the tutor's guidance more than three years. Although I did not perfectly master the swimming technique, however, I learnt something. As I remember, on 17-th year of the People's Republic (1928) I was the infantry company commander. Our regiment received an order to advance to the district of

Xingcheng for liquidation of a large bandit group. Yang Gong Su, the regiment commander, knew that I was a tough boy. He ordered me to make a reconnaissance and collect information about the enemy. I disguised myself as a peasant, put a mattock on a shoulder and went barefooted to the place where the bandit group was supposed to concentrate. When I was already coming back, I aroused suspicion of a mounted patrol of bandits. The riders galloped toward me, firing on the move. There was a river in front of me. As saying goes, "misfortune is the mother of wit". I threw away the mattock and plunged into water. I swam from the bank underwater and came to the surface to take a breath. At once several fires were shot and I dived again. And so it went on a few times. In that manner I managed to escape. Later I thought that if I had no knack of diving, I surely perished. The tutor told me that I had a strong character, therefore he used a hard method of training me to speed up the teaching process. If I was trained in an ordinary way, I would hardly get such a result.

It is necessary to start training in shallow water. Water level for those who can not swim must not be above the breast. If the current is strong and water level is above knees, a man stands unstably, if water level is above the navel, it is difficult to keep one's feet and if it is above the breast, a man falls down. It is necessary to take a small board, lie on it prone, hold on the board with one hand and make movements with the other, beat with force on water with both legs to keep the whole body in the horizontal position. You make movements with one arm and move forward. It is necessary to control your breath and to see to it that your body will not sink. When you are exhausted, stop, stand a little, take a rest, and train yourself again. In some time you may train you without the board. In that case you need to make movements with both arms in turn, your legs also beat on water surface in turn. Thanks to hand strokes and feet beats the body moves forward. The right arm simultaneously moves with your left leg, and the left arm, with your right leg. It is the simplest swimming method that is also called "the natural method", people call it "the dog-like swimming" (GOU PAO). This swimming technique allows a man to keep afloat for a long time and swim quite quickly at the same time. It is only necessary to put one shoulder a little forward, water resistance is less and speed is greater in that case.

Then, it is necessary to train a method of swimming on the back. After it the "trampling water technique" is trained: one needs to make movements with both arms in turn before the breast and "trample" water with both legs in turn, keeping the body in the vertical position. Arms and legs make circular movements. In that case the counter force that arises during arms and legs movements keeps the body on the surface and does not allow it to sink. Then method of "entering" water, that is "diving", is trained. That is the case when the whole body is under water. Push off with two feet from the bottom in shallow water, jump up, and dive into water. Make downward movements with arms and legs work in deep water, the body moves upward. If you change the direction of strokes and concentrate QI in the lower part of your stomach, your body starts sinking down. After lowering to the bottom of a water pool take the stance "Rider". It is necessary to hold breath, concentrate attention. At first, it is difficult to maintain a stable position, but gradually, at higher levels of training you can be in such a position for a long time, at that you must make movements with your arms. After some time you will be able "to sit" in such a position steadily for a long time.

After that it is necessary to train "walking on the bottom of a pool": bent your body in the waist, stretch arms forward and make movements with them backward in synchronization with leg movements (steps). It is one of the methods of movement under water, it is also called "swimming like a swine". For that, it is necessary to lower QI to DANTIEN. Then one can start to train the "pushing-off" method: it is the case when you "push off" with both legs, the upper part of the body is above water surface. In such a position you move forward as if you walk on a flat earth surface. Out of all swimming methods it is the most difficult one. At first, you raise one arm and make movements with the other, helping your legs. With time you will be able to raise the second arm and keep your body in water only with the help of legs only. At first, it is difficult to maintain the body in vertical position, you start drowning, but with time your head keeps above water, then come outward your shoulders and breast. It already is a good result. Some people even can achieve to come outward of the water surface up to their waist, but it is necessary to have inborn abilities to do that. I trained myself for several years, but I can keep only shoulders above water.

At last, "jumps" in water environment are trained. By that time the body becomes nimble, legs and arms are deft, moreover, if you also practise WU SHU, so a good foundation is laid. All those things will be needed in a combat with an enemy in water environment. The method is as follows: if you want "to jump" to the left, you need to row with both arms to the right, the torso is tilted to the left, the feet also push off to the right. If you want "to jump" to the right, you do similar actions to the opposite side. While jumping forward, you make movements

with both arms backward, your feet also push off backward. When jumping backward, you do all actions in the opposite direction. When jumping up, you make movements downward and at the same time bend both legs before the breast and abruptly straighten them to sides (to the left and to the right) and downward. QI must be concentrated in the region of the lungs at that. It is necessary to act in the opposite direction to sink down. When you acquire a required knack, you will easily make jumps in any direction: forward and backward, upward and downward, to the left and to the right. When you achieve such level of skill, you may regard your success to be quite considerable.

Preparation for a combat in water environment is based on the rule of four hicroglyphs: QI ("air", or "breath" in this context), YUE ("jump"), YAN ("eyes"), JIAN ("arrow"). QI involves a breath hold for a long time and water circulation through the nose, i.e. water is taken by the mouth and is let out through the nose. It is very difficult to do at first, sometimes it even causes a nose bleed. If you practise QI GONG (training of breath and the vital energy) at the same time, you will make a progress sooner. I, for example, trained myself during three years, but I can make only one or two rounds of circulation. YUE is jumps in water and we have already narrated about them in detail. YAN is eyes. It is necessary not only to open eyes in water, but also see somewhat father on. Special eyes training is needed to attain a good result. Training method is as follows: fill a wash-basin with cold clean water, sink your head into water and open your eyes. It is quite unpleasant at first, even some redness and swelling (of eyelids) can appear. After you get used to it, it is necessary to proceed to training in a water pool, first on surface, then in depth. If you can make out a small thing on the bottom

at a distance of 3 CHIs (about 1 m), the result is rather good. It is necessary to wash your eyes with good-quality tea after training. At my time I trained my eyes under water too zealously and because of it I saw everything as if in mist. At last, I was on the verge of losing my sight. I was treated at the Peking Central clinic. My sight restored in a month, but until now my left eye does not see quite distinctly. It shows that the way to mastership is very difficult. JIAN is "arrow". It concerns the effect of so-called "water arrow" upon the enemy. This method is as follows: both arms move backward, the palms turn upward and the arms move from the waist level to armpits, i.e. forward and upward. At that both legs push off downward and backward. At the same time, it is necessary to take some water into the mouth and sprinkle it on the enemy's face. If you stand on the bottom, those actions result in that some part of water before your breast move toward the enemy and pushes him at his breast, the enemy shifts backward and loses his balance. At that moment it is necessary to turn palms and make arm movements forward and downward and tilt the body backward. At the same time push off downward and forward with your feet. It will result in the enemy to be thrown away at a distance of 1 ZHANG (about 3.3 m). Also, water can be splashed at the enemy's face with hands on the water surface.

Using this description as a guide, one can master all kinds of swimming techniques. But mind and heart are needed to comprehend all these and in order to comprehend it you need practice, it is not enough just to read. One has to train oneself and everything will be all right.

20. Sluice Shutter Weighing 1000 JINs (QIAN JIN ZHA)

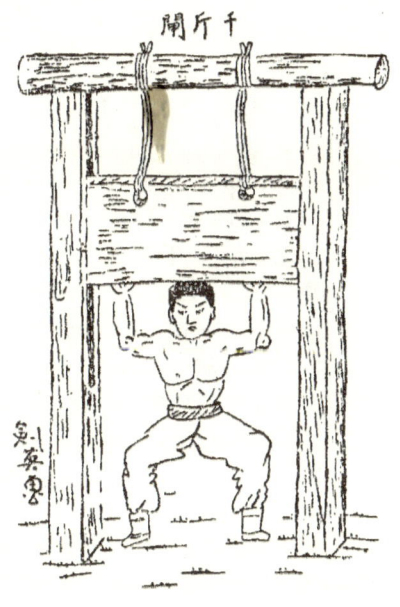

"Sluice Shutter weighing 1000 JINs" is a hard exercise strengthening the outside, it belongs to the hard force of YANG. If you look at a man doing this exercise, you can realize at once that this exercise develops the force of both arms perfectly well by weight-lifting. Actually, thanks to that a (heavy) weight is lifted, all three levels of the body (arms, torso, and legs) are trained. Unlike to several exercises for palms and fingers and other kinds of GONG FU which specialize in training certain body parts, all parts of the body are activated and work in coordination in this exercise.

The method of doing this exercise basically is quite simple. In it natural forces of a man are used to full extend, it is the most appropriate for their development. However, if you are a short man of slight build and extremely weak, it will be much more difficult for you to achieve good results in this exercise.

Training at the first stage does not require the use of any gadgets: legs in the stance of QI MA BU ("On horseback"), both hands are raised up high above the head, fingers are directed backward, palms face upward. This position is like that one in BA DUAN JIN ("Eight Pieces of Brocade") where it is called as "Raising the Earth and Returning (Adjusting) Three Heaters[41] to their Source". Through this exercise the "supporting" force is trained. After three month training a stone drum weighing 10-15 kg can be used for training, its weight should be gradually increased to 100 kg. When you are able to hold it during half an hour and longer and you don't gasp for breath and don't sweat, the drum can be replaced with a stone "sluice shutter". The "sluice shutter" should be put into slots specially made in two wooden posts set opposite each other. Prepare a few long rectangular stone slabs weighing 15 kg each and one big slab weighing 100 kg. Use at first the slab weighing 100 kg: put it into the slots of the posts and hang on braids (to a crossbar fixed at the top of the posts). The distance between the slab and the ground level must be 4 CHI (about 1.3 m); supports should be put to fix it in that position. It is necessary to squat under the slab for training and lift it up. One needs to estimate individual abilities while training and some time later add one light slab (weighing 15 kg), putting it into slots. By

---

Editor's notes:

[41] "Three Heaters" (SAN JIAO) in Chinese traditional medicine is a conventional organ that combines the functions of several organs. The upper heater summarizes the functions of the heart and the lungs in the distribution of QI and blood for nourishment of different organs and tissues. The middle heater summarizes the functions of the spleen and the stomach in digestion and absorption of nutrients. The lower heater summarizes the functions of the kidneys and bladder, controls water exchange and secretions.

adding slabs, increase gradually the weight. Finally, a trainee will be able to hold a weight of 250 kg and more. In such a way the utmost force is born in a man and finally you will get the ability to hold a weight of 1000 JINs (500 kg). In other words, you will be able to lift a weight of 1000 JINs with both arms at once! It is necessary to train yourself for a long time, without breaking for a day, to strengthen "primordial" ("natural", "born") forces. After successful completion of training not only both arms but also all body parts which equally participate in the exercise become strong. All muscles are strengthened and filled with force, and that is evident fact.

A great number of people on the North (of China) train this exercise along with other kinds of GONG FU. Real strength of northerners is quite close to that one of aliens[42], therefore this exercise by its nature is the most suitable to them. However, after coming to the South of China, the exercise also became one of the most favorite and esteemed arts it is regarded as one of the best kinds of GONG FU. This exercise is one of the main exercises for training force in Shaolin.

Editor's notes:

[42] In the text MANCHUN means non-Chinese people, aliens; in this context it seems to mean the Europeans who, as a rule, are bigger and stronger than the Chinese, especially inhabitants of Southern provinces.

21. Covering with a Gold Bell (JIN ZHONG ZHAO)

This exercise is a hard one, it strengthens both outside (muscles, bones, sinews) and inside (the inner organs). It is the most important hard exercise out of all 72 Arts. This exercise is rather complicated and difficult. It is necessary to make a mallet of stuff and strike with it on the whole surface of the body, on the front and the back. At first you will feel some pain but after training for a long time feeling of pain will gradually disappear. At that time the mallet of stuff can be replaced with a wooden one. When you feel no pain from blows, the wooden mallet can be replaced with an iron one. Bring to perfection until you feel no pain from blows. The gist of this method is similar to "Iron Shirt" (see par.#9) and "Iron Bull" (see par.#36).

If you practise this method for two or three years, your breast and your back will become strong like stone or iron; it is of no importance whether the enemy punches or kicks, it will do no harm. Even a sword blow will not do any injury to a man who practises the skill of "Gold Bell". Chest and back bones of that man become compacted like a single whole. It is necessary to use tinctures to cure bruises of muscles and bones after blows with mallets or falls (somersaults).

22. Exercise "Finger Lock" (SUO ZHI GONG)

It is a soft exercise that strengthens inside, it belongs to the soft force of YIN, but also develops the hard force of YANG at the same time. This specialized exercise for strengthening finger tips has great similarity to and some difference with such methods as "Force of Eagle Claws" (YING ZHAO LI) and "Making Holes in Stones" (DIAN SHI GONG). All those exercises form so called "Deadly 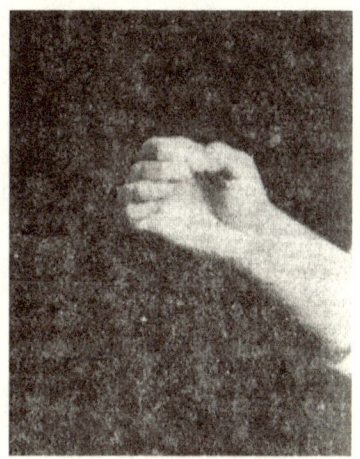 Arm" (SHA SHOU)[43]. Differences between them are given below. For instance, the exercise "Force of Eagle Claws" trains the force of fingers for locks and the exercise "Making Holes in Stones" trains the ability to deliver thrusts with finger tips. "Finger Lock" also trains finger tips for seizing movements but differs from two previous skills in training methods and methods of use.

Editor's notes:

[43] Hieroglyph SHA has a meaning "to kill", "deadly", "lethal" and also "hard", "rigid", "stiff".

Training method: at the first stage of mastering this skill, squeeze together two fingers – the middle finger and forefinger tightly and join them after bending to the bent thumb. All three fingers tightly join each other with their tips. A hollow is formed in the center of the palm, the spot between the thumb and the forefinger (HU KOU, literally "tiger's mouth") makes a circle. Press your fingers with force like a cook taking seasoning. Keep them a little in this position, then open and have a rest. Then, press tightly again with force. Do the exercise each day in your spare time without limiting number of repetitions. When pressing fingers, it is necessary to use the force of the whole arm, send it to the tips of three fingers, concentrate the Spirit and collect QI.

After one year of pertinacious training the lock will become strong. At that time, take a piece of board, 3 or 4 cm thick, squeeze it between fingers, continue to train you as before and try to press a hole through the board with fingers. It is the first step on the way to mastership and it may take more than two years, but it can take less than one year with diligence. Then, continue to train you as before with an iron plate. It is necessary to seek for the plate to be dented with fingers. Mastership reaches perfection at that stage. Four to five years of persistent training may pass from the start of familiarization with the exercise to its completion. If after successful mastering this GONG FU, you seize some part of the enemy's body with three fingers, you will surely crush his muscles or splinter his bones, inflicting a very severe wound on him.

23. Luohan's Exercise (LUOHAN GONG)

The Luohan's exercise is the inner exercise designed to improve the ability to see at night time. This is the purport of this exercise. This kind of GONG FU belongs to the Buddhist system of exercises designed to train the keenness of vision. This kind of training is quite difficult for an ordinary man, especially at the initial stage, but it results in the ability to see in pitch darkness. This exercise is designed, for example, for those who enter the army to serve at remote frontiers, perform noble deeds and stand on guard of justice. By employment of this technique in pitch darkness you can kill the enemy or mine a fortress under siege and carry out a sabotage to eliminate some outstanding person, for example a commander. Both eyes are to be trained, in that case you acquire the ability to see the smallest objects in pitch darkness. But for that, it is necessary to be the full success in doing exercises.

The following can be recommended as a preliminary exercise on the way to acquiring this art: it is necessary to assume the stance MA BU ("Rider") each night and look at the moon. In my childhood I had poor eyesight, after having started to train "Contemplation of the Moon", I noted some time later that my eyesight had been improving. I then resorted to the help of my second tutor who taught me training methods of "Night Vision" and auxiliary exercises. Although I did not perfectly acquire this art, I could not only avert further deterioration of my eyesight, but significantly improved it.

Training method. The lesson can be divided into several parts. Each time, when you wake up, don't open the eyes. Rub thumbs of both hands with each other until you feel hot, then rub your eyes (with the back side of the thumbs) 14 times. With the eyes remaining to be shut, roll your eyes seven times (from the left leftward-upward, strictly upward, rightward-upward, then rightward and rightward-downward, then strictly downward, leftward-downward and leftward). It is included into the complex of exercises for children TONG ZI GONG[44] and called "the skill of opening and closing eyes", "rolling with eyes". After finishing to roll eyes do not open them for some time, then open the eyes, but not too wide. Massage points QUAN ZHU[45] on the brows with projected bent joints of thumbs 70 times. Then, rub cheek-bones with your hands and rub the back of the ears – points ER GEN[46] 36 times with circular movements. Then rub the forehead with your hands, start from the center and move along both brows, as if a hairdresser is combing or arranging hair, reach the end of the hair on your back, do so 72 times. Swallow a great amount of saliva in your mouth. This exercise for health sake is carried out immediately after sleep.

Editor's notes:

[44] TONG ZI GONG, a complex of exercises for development of child's organism primarily designed for the development and mobility of joints, sinews and muscles.
[45] Points QUAN ZHU are on the inner part of brows beside the nose.
[46] Points ER GEN (ER HOU) – the lower back of the ear.

A torch (lantern) with a shade of light green paper is also used, the lantern is filled with aromatic oil. The flame should be small. Put the lantern at the dark part of the room. Stand before the lantern at a distance of 6 or 7 meters approximately or sit with your bent knees, or sit at a bench, calm down and adjust your breath, pluck up your spirits, look at the lantern. Look at fire, when your eyes are tired, close them and exercise opening and closing eyes and eye roll as described above, do rolling to the left and to the right. Train yourself each night and in the morning, do the exercises during one hour.

Replace the lantern shade with that one of darker color after three month training and increase the distance by 30-60 cm. Change each day from brighter to darker color up to dark blue and stop at that (don't change color). Then increase gradually the distance from 6-7 meters to 30 meters. When the size of the flame from a horse bean turns to a soybean, stop at that. At that time, extend morning training up to two hours. After reaching that stage, it will be possible to clearly discern various objects at dark time of the night. Continue to train you diligently and persistently and in that case you will be able to see unmistakably a man at a distance of 35 meters. With that LUOHAN GONG kind of GONG FU is considered as acquired. After successful acquirement of this kind of GONG FU that is also called "The Art of Night Vision" you will see at night almost as well as at day time. "Swimming Art" (QIU SHUI SHU) also includes some exercises for eyes, but the these exercises are basic ones, as they improve in addition the ability to see under water, therefore one can not help but train this exercise. It is reasonable that there is such a saying in the province of Jiangsu:

"If you perfectly acquired the skill of ZAO ZI[47], you tower over the enemy in a combat like a mountain peak". By ZAO ZI masters from the province of Jiangsu allegorically meant an eyeball. Each day, before taking meal, it is necessary to eat a small amount of mutton liver boiled in water and improve periodically with it the inside (the internal organs).

Editor's notes:

[47] ZAO ZI, a fruit of the Chinese Date.

24. Lizard Climbs the Wall (BI HU YU QIANG SHU)

"Lizard Climbs the Wall" is an exercise that develops the external softness and the internal hardness. It can be found under another name PA BI - "Climbing a Wall" or GUA HUA – "A Hanging Picture". After acquiring this skill a trainee can "glue" his back to a wall and move on the wall in any direction by using the force directed to his elbows. If a trainee demonstrates the desire to learn and will, he will be able to move on walls as easily as a lizard can do. A lizard has two names – "BI HU" or "SHOU GONG", but sometimes "lizard" in the name is changed with "scorpion" (XIE HU), therefore the name of this exercise is conventional in many respects.

It is not easy to learn this art. Only two or three men out of a hundred who start to acquire the movements succeed in mastering the technique to perfection. The procedure of the exercise is as follows: it is necessary to lie on the back with the face upward, lean the elbows on the surface with the use of muscles, raise your body and fix it that position. Then, it is

necessary to move, just as a skolopendra jumps, applying force, on the surface with jerks to the side to which your head is turned.

There are the following methods which can be called as methods that help to perfectly acquire this art. During the first year or even during two years some disciples can only move on the surface, coiling like a snake, and only after acquirement of this part they start to train this exercise on a brick wall. The surface of the wall should not be smooth, it should have both concave and convex parts. Concave parts can be one CHI (30 cm) long and convex, up to one CUN (3 cm). A training method for this art is as follows: it is necessary to press elbows and forearms to a wall, the back as if is glued to it, take a deep breath with the stomach, draw in the breast to make the chest as flat as possible[48], and start gradually moving. At first, it is not advisable to overcome more than one or two bricks. Don't worry about injuring your feet, it is necessary to count your movements.

Those who have been learning this kind of art for a long time must have received a positive experience. If they were not lazy in the process of learning, they are capable of moving on uneven vertical surface downward and upward as well. Later on

---

Editor's notes:

[48] At that the center of gravity will shift to the lower part of the stomach, which makes the task significantly easier.

- 132 -

they will be able to acquire the technique of movement to the right and to the left.

For easier movement on a wall, the body can be rubbed with lead or sand. To achieve the best result, it is recommended to use a mixture of sand, lead, and pig blood to rub into the body. In that case a trainee will move on a wall comparatively easy.

To make the training process more complicate, one can knock on bulges of the wall to smooth the surface, level both bulging and concave parts. It is better to use a mixture of lead and sand when the wall becomes extremely smooth. When all those means are employed, movements of a trainee will not differ from those ones of a lizard on a wall. It is necessary to train oneself persistently during ten years without stopping for a minute. Training can be finished only when the highest level of skill is reached.

25. The Art of Lash (BIAN JIN FA)

The purport of "The Art of Lash" is to prepare both forearms for strong pressure. Unlike "The Art of the Iron Arm" which aims are similar to it and when forearms are also trained by striking blows, this exercise employs pressure with forearms on a hard surface.

A wooden stick can be used when you just start to cope with this exercise. It is necessary to lean with both forearms on the straight, horizontally placed, wooden stick and press on it with all your force, the body slightly rises at that. When your waist has risen about the height of the stick, it is necessary to fix this position for some time and then lower yourself to the ground slowly. The wooden stick must be fixed on two poles at a sufficient height. You should train yourself each day in the morning and in the evening. The exercise must be done by series, it is necessary to rise and lower oneself ten times in each series. Number of series must be gradually increased.

If a sharp pain is felt in your arms, tumors and swelling are formed on the forearms, you should cure yourself with "medical elixir" (YAO SHUI). It should be used as follows: rub "medical elixir" onto your forearms and hands before and after training. That medicine can be also used to prevent pain feeling.

After one-year training when your arms get used to pressure on thick objects, it will be easier to proceed to training with bamboo sticks. It is necessary to prepare suitable gadgets to train oneself with bamboo sticks. Drive into the earth four heavy piles arranged like legs of a table so that the rectangular space was limited by them. Each pile must be made of very thick bamboo (MAO ZHU). As soon as it is done, four or five such sticks of MAO ZHU should be laid on the piles so that they lie as flat as possible, parallel to the ground, and tightly tied to the piles like a table top to its legs. A soft rope is the best thing to be used for fixing. A trainee takes the position MA BU ("Horse Stance"), leans with his forearms on the horizontal bamboo and presses on it with a very great force for some time, then has a little rest and starts to do the exercise again.

As soon as you start to train yourself with bamboo, the bamboo sags one or two CUNs[49], not more. However, with time, the force of pressure will start to increase. The result is regarded as attained only when you are capable of pressing down (sagging the bamboo) to six or seven CUNs. At that stage one more layer of bamboo stems must be fixed above the bamboo on which

---

Editor's notes:

[49] CUN, a Chinese traditional measure of length. One CUN is equal to 1/30 of a meter (about 3.3 cm).

you pressed before and continue to do the exercise; tie above one more (layer) after some time. Up to ten layers of bamboo stems can be added in such a way, training can be finished only when you will be able press down not to 6 or 7 CUNs as before, but to one CHI[50] approximately. It takes three or four years for the most of trainees to get that knack, only then learning that GONG FU can be regarded as finished.

After it, you can proceed to pressure on stones, it should be trained to such a state when pressure on stones becomes so strong that they will begin to crumble and dents will appear in them.

This skill is the following purpose: you will be able to beat off blows with JIAN sword, knife, or lash without worrying about injuries. Men who reach mastership do not kill enemies for no particular reason, preferring only to stop them. This art will also prove to be useful if you are taken prisoner and your arms are tied: there will be no traces on the skin, even from a thick rope.

---

[50] CHI, also a Chinese traditional measure of length. One CHI is equal to 1/3 of a meter (about 33 cm).

26. Exercise "PIPA" (PIPA GONG)

The exercise "PIPA" is also called SAN YIN ZHI – "Three Fingers of Yin" and ZHI TOU TAN - "Springy Fingers". This exercise is specialized on strengthening the outer side of finger tips and nails. It is a "hard" exercise belonging to the YANG force, a special exercise for the development of the "flicking" force of fingers.

When training fingers (in other exercises), one finger, either the forefinger or the middle finger, is often used. In the exercise "PIPA" four fingers which do springy movements (flicks) in turn are used. It resembles playing PIPA, the Chinese guitar: as if fingers run over strings, hence that name of the exercise. It is necessary to do flicks with finger nails with force; however, one should try to do those

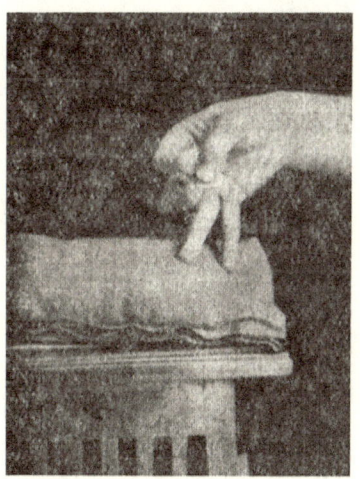

operations softly enough and as a result you will master the "soft" part of the exercise. When you succeed in training this ("soft") part, it will be enough for keeping the enemy in check efficiently. They say, it seems to be simple, but only that who really seeks to reach mastership and shows endurance for a long time will get a good result. It is unlike other kinds of "hard" skills in which it is as easy as pie to get good results.

However, one can not help but resort to medicines, one has to eliminate shortcomings by some auxiliary means too. Follow the given recipe for training, select required components and use it externally: mix white vinegar and white salt, 5 kg each component, put them into a caldron and heat for one hour. Then, remove sediments from the mixture, add 5 kg of sand from a lake, put that into a stone mortar and pound into small particles, fill a bag of thick fabric with obtained powder. Put the bag on a strong wooden bench, smooth the bag out and wait until it becomes dry and hard, turning into one piece. After that it can be used.

Training method: lay tightly all five fingers in the region of nails and do springy flicks with four fingers in turn with force. Start from the forefinger, then the middle finger, the ring finger, the little finger follow, again the little finger, the ring finger, the middle finger and the forefinger. Continue to do the exercise in such a manner. Hit the bag 108 times each day, in the morning and in the evening. After three-year training you will be able to get results. If you deliver a blow at the enemy by means of a "flick", the effect will be different from that one of "Diamond Finger" or other techniques with which the chest or the stomach can be pierced, but it will be enough to subdue the enemy. At the same time this technique can be employed so that it will lead to inevitable death (of the enemy) and no medicine can save him. After hitting the enemy no traces are seen outside, but a severe injury is inflicted inside. This method as well as the exercise "Finger like Spring" and all other kinds of YIN hand methods belong to so called methods of "Wolfish Poison"

(LANG DU)[51], therefore there is a ban on transfer of this knack to ordinary people among fighters. That one who trains this skill has outer distinctive peculiarities: the nails of his four fingers that did the exercise are of black color, and owing to that nail blackness he differs from ordinary (people). At the same time (the color of) his thumb nail that is not used in the exercise is like that one of an ordinary man. Poor QI and blood circulation after training for a long time according that method accounts for that, this phenomenon appears on the people who practice this method. When you meet an enemy, you can know his technique from the above indications and be on guard. If you don't master the skill of the "YIN Hand", you should politely bow and leave, otherwise you can be seriously wounded.

Although this skill belongs to "hard" force of Yang, the exact tool of QI is softness Yin, and if those two principles are linked, the skill will be superb. One must not bring the situation to a threat of life or injuries, one must not abuse this skill. Otherwise, by striking ("flicking") with two fingers, a man can be wounded so that he will not be able to restore his health. There is the demand for modesty in the "Secret Virtue" YIN DE[52] and a combatant, training that difficult exercise, must always keep it in mind.

Editor's notes:

[51] LANG DU has an additional meaning – "cruelty", "treachery".
[52] YIN DE has an additional meaning – feminine, passive element of the nature, female virtue.

27. The Pole of a Falling Star (LIU XING ZHUANG)

The exercise "The Pole of a Falling Star" belongs to hard external exercises, it develops the hard YANG force. The training method is very simple. Dig a thick bamboo trunk[53] into the ground, wrap tightly the outside of it with a thick hemp cord. Stand before the pole and deliver different types of blows ("pushing", "striking", "cutting" etc.) with your head, fists, palms, shoulder joints, elbows, wrists, forearms, legs and buttocks at the bamboo pole. Everything is the same as in the exercise "Striking the Paper Block" (DA ZHI DUN, see details in par.#3, exercise "1000 Layers of Paper"): using various methods, imagine an enemy before you and deliver blows at his several parts of the body. It is the initial stage of the exercise. If you train yourself hard for a long time and adhere to constancy, your skin and muscles gradually become thick and strong, feeling of pain caused by doing the exercise will disappear and the spirit which was shapeless will strengthen. All parts of the body will become as if made of iron and it will be of no importance in a bout if you strike with an arm or a legs. If you diligently and assiduously exercise for three years, you will realize that a positive result has been achieved.

Editor's notes:

[53] Trunks of some species of bamboo reach 25 to 30 cm in diameter.

A great number of people in northern provinces practise this kind of GONG FU. Sometimes it is called "Standing like a pile and beating a pile" (ZHAN ZHUANG DA ZHUANG). Actually this exercise at the initial stage can be trained at any suitable place and at any convenient time. It helps to develop body, arms, eyes, and movements at most.

28. Poles of Plum Bloom (MEI HUA ZHUANG)

The exercise "Poles of Plum Bloom" is a "soft" and "internal" kind of GONG FU that develops the whole body. Furthermore, it forms a base for acquirement of the skill "Flinging on the Cornice and Climbing the Wall" (FEI YAN ZOU BI). The exercise is done on poles and thanks to that lightness of the body, mobility and dexterity of movements are trained, the exactness of leaps and skipping along (poles) are perfected. There are other names for "Poles of Plum Bloom", they are "Poles of Seven Stars" (QI XING ZHUANG) and "Poles of Nine Stars" (JIU XING ZHUANG)[54]. After successful acquirement of the exercise you can use that skill in dangerous situations and in a combat. Besides training leaps, the exercise is very important for eyes[55].

At the first stage the exercise does not require to climb poles. Instead of it, paint plum blossoms on the ground with lime, the pattern of petal arrangement must exactly correspond to the pattern of actual pole arrangement. The distance between poles (and between petals respectively) should be 2 to 3 CHIs (0.66 m to 1 m). Each "blossom" consists of five small circles arranged

---

Editor's notes:

[54] Number of poles (7 or 9) or their arrangement resembling, for instance, an arrangement of petals in a plum blossom and so like, account for all the names.
[55] Literally "Force of eyes" in the text.

as petals of the flower, that is on the circumference. Neighboring "blossoms" are equally spaced, about one CHI (0.33 m). The diameter of a small circle is about 3 CUNs (about 10 cm), it should not be too big. After "plum blossoms" have been painted, one "petal" inside each flower should be marked as a "false" pole, the other are marked with symbols or figures. The trainee stands on a "petal" inside one of the "blossoms", he puts one foot, directs force into the toe of the foot and takes a stance on one leg in the position of a "sentry". From here on one can oneself choose the sequence and the direction of skipping along (poles), for instance, to the left 3, to the right 4, forward 2, backward 5 and so on. You skip along according a chosen procedure. The left and right legs make movements at will, pushing off and landing on a foot which is more convenient for you. It would be still better if somebody who is standing besides you will give commands by voice. Move according to the commands. For example, the man who gives commands loudly shouts: "Blossom two, pole one!". You immediately must jump to the right and reach the first "pole" of the second "blossom". Continue doing in the same manner. The only requirement is not to step on "empty" ("false") pole in each "blossom". When you step on a pole, the toe of the foot should be exactly at the center of a circle without shifting to any side.

When you learn to steadily and easily move on the blossoms painted on the ground, you can gradually proceed to training with real poles. It is much more difficult: if you shift the torso aside even a little bit, the supporting leg will not be able to keep the balance and you will fall down. Even if you do not fall down, all the same the torso will be unsteady and will not stay firm and your movements will be constrained and uncertain.

- 143 -

Therefore, it is necessary to pay close attention to the first stage. When you just start training with poles, while walking at will, it is impossible to maintain the proper positions. Therefore, it is necessary to move on four real poles in one "blossom" in the beginning, then proceed to training with eight poles in two "blossoms" etc. If you gradually make the exercise more complicate in such a manner, you will be able to eliminate many shortcomings and overcome difficulties of the initial stage. Keep in mind: it is allowable to proceed to training with poles only when you learn to easily and freely move on the ground. If you are not able to move on the ground, how can you stand on the poles?

The poles are to be made of hard wood, their length should be 3.5 CHIs (about 1.16 m). The top of the poles are flat and the lower part with a diameter of 2 CUNs (about 6.66 cm) is narrower. Dig poles at the places where petals of plum blossoms were painted, the narrower side down so that they stick out from the ground to a height of 1.5 CHI approximately (about 50 cm). The upper surface of the poles (the butt-end) must be smooth and even (flat). But do not forget about leaving one "false" pole in each "blossom" which must be driven to the ground only to 1 or 2 CUNs (3.33 – 6.66 cm.). If the earth is mellow, it will be loose and can fall down, if you do not stand on it firmly. Such a "false" pole must be available in each "blossom", its arrangement is arbitrary. The trainee has to mark (number) the poles in order to avoid confusion and after choosing movement sequence he has to do the exercise according to the above-mentioned procedure. It is necessary to attain the ability to freely and firmly move on the poles and do it quickly and easily. Pole height may be increased after that, but all poles must be of the same height. Then barriers of barbed

wire and other sharp and cutting things may be arranged around the poles and pole height may be increased to 3 CHIs (about 1 m) or more up to the maximum height. It would be a good thing to put on loads such as small bag with sand for training, but sand should be pre-heated and soaked in swine blood and be used after that. Otherwise, your blood can be easily spoiled. Copper rings on legs or coins of base metal may be also used, three years of hard training can give some results. When you achieve mastership, the body will become energetic, movements will become easy and active. If you engage an enemy, you will be able to find instability in the enemy, find gaps in his defense and smash him.

As far as the exercises "Poles of Seven Stars", "Poles of Nine Stars", "Three-Row Poles", "Poles of Nine Temples", and exercises on bricks put on the butt-end (YI SHAN ZHUANG FA) are concerned, all their patterns and methods as a whole are similar to those of the above-mentioned. But the best method of training is training on poles, therefore it is no need to repeat it again. A trainee himself has the right to choose a training method.

29. The Art of Stone Padlock (SHI SUO GONG)

Much clearer and louder were these sounds in the past than now, but no place can be found to enjoy them at present...

"The Art of Stone Padlock" serves to strengthen the external power, brings strength to the body, like that one of the sun. This method serves to harden arms. It is especially suitable for lifting some heavy things. The efficiency of this art is not inferior to that one of the method of the "Iron Bag" (TIE DAI GONG). The shape and the outline of the "Stone Padlock" are similar to those ones of a common copper padlock. That padlock has a U-shaped bar and a barrel, but has no hole for the key.

It is necessary to take a stone MA (MA SHI) or a stone QING (QING SHI) to acquire this technique. The weight of a small stone padlock must be 20 JINs[56] at least and the weight of the biggest padlock may be 60 to 70 JINs[57]. At first, one has to learn to lift such a stone padlock with an arm and hold it suspended. The exercise is done with each arm in turn. Take a stone

---

Editor's notes:

[56] JIN, a Chinese traditional measure of weight. 1 JIN is equal to 0.5 kg. Thus, the weight of the stone is about 10 kg.
[57] That corresponds to 30 to 35 kg after conversion into the common measure of weight.

padlock with a hand and fix the hand at the level of your breast (the arm is straight in the elbow joint). Bend the arm in the wrist so that the fist that holds the stone padlock should be pointed up. Do the exercise many times. The aim of this exercise is to make the arm strong. After finishing this exercise, raise and lower the arm so that the fist should move up and down in the vertical plane (the arm is straight in the elbow). You may imagine a vertical line, for example, on a wall where you stare and move the fist with the stone padlock along that line. Stop the raising arm only when the arm and the shoulder will make one (horizontal) line. The arm must be as if hanging in emptiness. After assimilating and consolidating main principles, do the exercise with turns of the body in the region of your waist and other movements simultaneously. After that, start to throw up the padlock. Raise, lower and move up abruptly your arm with force. Try to achieve the stone padlock to fly up and rotate round its axis in the air, making, at any rate, two or three revolutions, then catch it for the U-shaped bar with your hand. It is necessary to achieve such a state when you are able to control the number of revolutions, increase or decrease their number (revolutions) by will. With time your arms will harden and the force in them will achieve a certain amount.

It is not worth trying to make too many revolutions of the padlock in the air at the beginning. You will be in perfect command of this art only when you have trained the rotation technique to the ideal level, then you will not be able to do harm to your body when training (further) this exercise.

After finishing with the rotation technique of a stone padlock, start to acquire the technique of "accepting" a falling stone on a stretched hand. When training that, learn to throw a stone up

and catch it, its trajectory being a vertical line. The purport of the exercise is as follows. Throw up a stone padlock so that it should reach the level of your head crown, and then fall down vertically. Set the back of a clenched fist under the falling stone padlock as if you divided the stone into two halves (i.e. the fist must be under the center of gravity of the stone padlock), at the same time lower the palm of the other arm on the U-shaped bar from above and press it to the fist. Continue your work with the stone padlock in the same manner: throw it up at first, then catch it. Do not squeeze the stone padlock in your hand, but accept it on the fist. When your shoulders, elbow joints and fingers become strong, it will mean that you are on the way to perfection in this art. Now the execution of this exercise needs to be improved by multiple repetition of the learnt movements.

The back can be divided into two halves, the right one and the left one. Muscles of the left part account for the left arm and the right one for actions of the right arm. Take a stone padlock with the right hand, throw it up behind the back from your waist so that it could be caught on the level of the left shoulder, catch the stone padlock near the left shoulder with your arm stretched. Turn the whole body to the left at that. Do the same with the left arm. Do not apply too great effort in the process of strengthening arms. Take care of your sides and your waist. If you ignore that and apply too great force, you may feel pain in the body.

After finishing the work with back muscles, start to train the waist. This exercise can also be done to the left side and to the right side. Lift a stone padlock with your right arm, start the movement from the right part of the waist (small of the back) and from the left part to the left side to throw a stone up. The

body should be also turned to the left and a thrown stone padlock be caught just in that position. Do the same with the other arm. After assimilating everything, finishing to learn the exercise and hardening the waist, it is necessary to unite both mentioned methods into one. In the process of exercising trainees may count movements to do them equally to the left and to the right.

When the first stage of training comes to the end, one may start to repeat all parts, gradually moving from the simple to the difficult and sparing a long time for it. At first, it is necessary to exercise with a stone padlock of 20 JINs (10 kg), then take a heavier one and gradually proceed to the stone padlock weighing 60 JINs (30 kg).

When learners assimilate this skill completely, they will be able to lift things weighing 100 to 300 JINs (50 – 150 kg). It is necessary to pay equal attention to both arms without leaving one arm inactive in the process of acquiring the skill. It will take about two years to acquire this skill. Only after that time you can be told to have attained a high level. It is easier to learn this art in childhood and later repeat and improve the knack of lifting, throwing up and pushing things of impressive weight easily.

30. Skill of the Iron Arm (TIE BI GONG)

"The skill of the Iron Arm" serves for strengthening both the "inner" and the "outer" as well as for the development of the force YANG. It is designed for training arms. The method of acquirement of this skill is very simple and presents no difficulties from the technical point of view. It is necessary to train oneself at the initial stage in the following manner: you has to strike at poles indoors with your arms, both with the outer and back side of an arm. Each day number of blows and their force should be increased. Thus, arms will be gradually strengthening.

With arm blows acquired, you should proceed to brushing up your skill. It is necessary to go on exercising both on wooden poles and trees. Trees should not be smooth and even like ice. They should be shaggy by touch, their surface should be uneven, bulging in some places and concave at other places. After training the technique, some time later, swells will appear on your skin, pain feeling in arms will be possible.

If you train you each day during a year, your arms will be so strong that you will be able to break wooden things and stone poles. At first, train you by striking at smooth and even things and then, with time, proceed to training with stones with rough (uneven) surface. A blow should be made as if deep down into or "through" a stone. Raise your arm, make a swing and hit with all your force so that a stone should be split to pieces.

After the acquirement of the technique your arms will become as strong as iron. It will be able to hit a man so that his bones will be broken and the internal organs will be severely injured. It will be easy to protect oneself with this arms from enemy's blows delivered with sword, knife or stick. Furthermore, with this arms you can push away, move and break various things. It will be possible to "break open the gate"[58] with one arm, without waiting for a moment when you will be defeated.

This technique is very useful and it will take relatively little time to learn it. Its essentials can be learnt within a year and mastered to perfection within three years. During a whole year the perfection of this technique can be matched with learning other methods of WU SHU. In the process of acquiring this method learners strengthen both the "inner" and the "outer". If you consolidate and repeat this technique during one year, your arms will obtain constant hardness, it will be possible to break with them not only a thin tree, but also a thick one, and arm blows will become of abrupt, chopping character.

Editor's notes:

[58]The meaning here is that is possible to force the enemy's defenses with powerful blows and win without waiting for an enemy's attack.

31. Fist like a Bullet (DAN ZI QUAN)

The exercise "Fist like a Bullet"[59] is a hard external exercise, it belongs to the YANG force. It is designed for perfecting blows at the enemy with the joints of the second finger phalanges set forward as regard to the front surface of a fist. It is also one of the methods of "Deadly Arm".

The training method is quite simple and resembles the exercise "Saddle" (MA AN GONG). But the exercise "Saddle" trains the force of the front striking surface of a fist and this exercise, finger joints. The hand is not completely clenched into fist, the fingers in the first phalange bend and take their place near the third joints (i.e. under the joints of the third phalanges, at the edge of a palm from the finger side). Fingers are not completely clenched into fist. The inner part of the hand (from the palm side) forms a plane. The thumb, bending, is

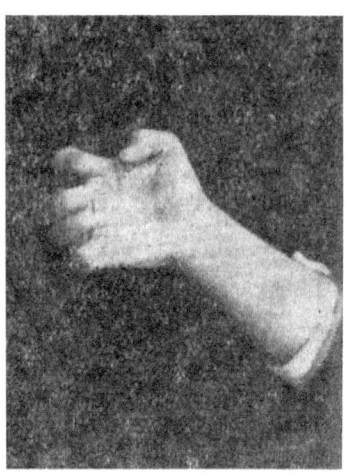

Editor's notes:

[59] One of the hieroglyphs in the name of this exercise has two readings and different senses; the second reading is TAN, a spring.

placed in the central part of the palm. The hand position is like that one during a seizure of an enemy's arm in the technique CHIN NA (Shaolin art of grappling with simultaneous press at vulnerable points). After the acquirement of proper shaping of the hand position, deliver blows forward, using the joints. At the first stage, it is necessary to deliver blows as if with a chisel on the surface of a flat wooden board. When a blow is hit, the elbow is bent and accompanies the fist, this movement should be made with the use of the energy XU ("to collect", "to accumulate"). Unlike the exercise "Saddle", the arm for a blow must not be kept straight (straightened, unbent) by stretching it. The man who has acquired the use of finger joints is capable of inflicting an injury to the enemy by hitting his muscles, but there are extremely few such people. An exceptionally effective ("strong" in the original text) "weapon" can be formed thanks to this exercise, what is called "to overpower hardness with hardness". However, it is not unquestionable in all cases, too great zeal or excessive training can lead to injuries, especially at the first stage, during the first few months. Therefore, when you start (to train) hands, you must be attentive and careful. It is necessary to start from the simple and the easy and gradually proceed to the complicated and the difficult. Avoid the danger (of injuries) arising from ardent aspiration for mastership. It is necessary to wash hands once with tinctures each day, before and after the exercise.

The first stage of training will result in a depression made in the wooden board after many blows. Then, it is necessary to take a stone and continue to train yourself as before. When a depression appears in the stone, take a steel plate. The natural property of a stone is solidity (hardness), a steel plate is still stronger and, additionally it has such a quality as elasticity.

Therefore, training in "hardness" must also include "soft" effort. The ability to chisel a depression in a steel plate with finger joints shows that a high level of the skill has been achieved. But it needs four or five years of stubborn training at least to attain that. This GONG FU also belongs to the section "Deadly Arm", but it is more effective as compared with the skills of "Finger Lock" (SUO ZHI GONG) and "Making Holes in Stones" (DIAN SHI GONG). In many methods fingers are used, but in this case joints are employed. Joints have no other practical use except hitting the enemy[60]. After the successful end of training you will be able to deliver a blow so hard that it will be fatal to the enemy. In a peaceful situation one must not have even a desire to injure a man, that's why a trainee who has acquired this method well must be always cautious and careful. Under no circumstances should you, if you rely on your skill, behave rudely and arrogantly, you will not, then, happen to injure a man because of reckless or careless behavior. Forerunners said: "Harm can be done suddenly and accidentally, those who learn martial techniques must be very watchful". One can injure bones by a blow after learning this skill during one year. It is similar to the method "Bone Injury" (XIE GU) of the style "Tiger's Claws" (HU ZHAO QUAN).

Editor's notes:

[60] To all appearances, it means that fingers can be also used for seizures and pressing on painful points, whereas bent joints are exclusively employed for blows.

32. Exercise "Soft Bones" (ROU GU GONG)

The exercise "Soft Bones" is the soft GONG FU of the internal force. It is called "Twisting the waist and bending the legs" in common speech. It is obligatory for training the "soft" GONG FU for those who practise WU SHU (Martial Arts). It allows to obtain flexibility of all joints, nimbleness and deftness of the body, avoid awkwardness and restraint of movements. First of all, it is necessary to start from training legs (LIU TUI). There is a saying among specialists in WU SHU: "You will not achieve a success in the course of your life if you practise Martial Arts without training legs". What does it mean – training legs LIU TUI? It means to kick. At that the supporting leg is strained and filled with the internal force and a striking leg is straight, it should fling above the head. It is necessary to kick with both legs in turn, train yourself in the morning and in the evening. One hundred kicks with each leg at least must be done during one training spell.

After half a year of such training one may proceed to the exercise "Bench facing the sky" (CHAO TIEN DENG). It is done in the following way: the supporting leg is straight; raise the other leg forward and up, press it to your ribs with arms, the sole of the foot faces up, the foot is near the ear. Train both legs in turn. Splits can be made as soon as several months pass. Splits are of two kinds, side and longitudinal splits. The side splits are made in the following way: legs are moved to the left and to the right until you sit (on the floor), the upper part of the body is straight all the time. To make longitudinal splits, legs are moved forward and back. If your left leg is in front and the right one behind, the front part of the right leg (hip and shank) and the calf of the left leg touch the floor, and vice versa if the right leg is in front and the left is behind.

All the above-said concerns leg training. Now let's talk about waist training. First of all, it is necessary to acquire the following exercises: "The cat stretches itself from a sleep" (LI MAO SHEN YAO), "The Grand Duke raises a tripod" (BA WAN JUI DING), "The Celestial bows" (XIAN REN ZUO YI). Stand at attention, interlace fingers of both hands and raise them above your head, then bend the upper part of your body until the palm touches the floor. Your legs should be absolutely straight at that, the slightest bend is not allowable. Your head, shoulders, and back are in one (vertical) plane. It is necessary to maintain such a posture during 20 to 30 minutes, then straighten oneself and have a rest. After it the waist has to be trained, that is to be bent and unbent. That's done in the following way: tilt the upper part of your body back and lean with your palms on the floor. The body takes the shape of a bridge. Then (also from the standing position), tilt the upper part of the body to the left and to the right. With time the body will become soft like cotton wool. The waist and the leg will become very flexible. You may roll yourself up into a ball in a lying position. You will be much more flexible than ordinary people. If you learn WU SHU on this base, certainly, you will achieve a great success.

Before training you may take a caldron, pour boiled water into it, cover with white fabric from above. When water cools down a little, lie on your back, steam your waist: the effect will be still better.

33. Exercise "Frog" (HAMA GONG)

This exercise is also called "Lifting a Stone Block". It belongs to the hard GONG FU, trains the external power and belongs to the YANG category. The purport of the exercise is to make muscles hard, which helps to beat off an enemy's attack. It is similar to the exercise "Iron Shirt" (TIE BU SHAN). Many people in the city of Tiantsin practise this exercise. Unfortunately, they simply "pump up" muscles. For instance, they lift weight of 30, 40, 50, 60, 70 and 90 kg. It is the most primitive method of training, the development of the internal force is out of question with this. This kind of GONG FU should be gradually acquired, don't hurry at no event. At first, wrists are trained, then shoulders and chest, then legs. This method approximates to the "soft" GONG FU, as it also trains the inner power, but force is emphasized in this case. It is unlike "Water Separation" (FEI SHUI GONG) in GONG FU where QI is the main thing and force is an addition.

It is the best to use a stone block for training a wrist. When lifting a weight, force must be concentrated in the wrist. Force will increase with time and muscle grow stronger. If you can lift a weight of 50 kg without appreciable effort, you can continue training without any gadgets. Concentrate force in your arms by clenching and unclenching fists, muscles will tighten at that. Then, clench fists firmly and turn their back side down, concentrate force in the region of the back of your head and neck. Force shifts are like a swing. Concentrate force in your shoulders after it. Move your shoulders back and concentrate

force in the chest, the chest muscles will tighten at that. When you acquire this to perfection, it will mean that your upper part of the body has been well trained. Next, the middle part of the body, that is the stomach region, should be trained. The nature of this method is similar to the exercises "Iron Bull" (TIE NIU GONG) and "Iron Shirt" (TIE BU SHAN). When muscles become stronger and hard, it is necessary to continue to improve in training "concentration of force".

After finishing to train the middle part of the body, it is necessary to proceed to training the lower part, that is the waist and the legs. For that, it is necessary to take the stance "Rider" each day and remain in it until you exhaust. Have a rest and take the stance "Rider" again. The time of staying in the stance must be gradually increased. It is necessary to train oneself until muscles become strong. In that case you will be able to concentrate force in any part of the body and even stabs of swords and spears can do you no harm. Specialists in WU SHU say about this kind of GONG FU: "That is training frog QI inside and muscle outside". Although it is the "hard" GONG FU by its nature, which trains the external power (muscle force), but partly it is also the "soft" GONG FU that develops and uses the internal energy. Besides, this method helps to cure illnesses and prolong life time.

34. Exercise "Piercing the Curtain" (CHUAN LIAN GONG)

The exercise "Piercing the Curtain" is the "soft" GONG FU, it trains the internal energy and belongs to the section "Skill of Light Body" (QING SHEN GONG). The purport of it lies in the ability to make horizontal leaps like a swallow's flight. We often see performances of roaming acrobats who show leaps through rings with daggers or burning torches on the ring perimeter. That is just a demonstration of that kind of GONG FU. The audience see: one leap and an acrobat already passed through the ring with daggers or burning torches on the edges. It seems to be simple and easy. Nobody thinks about the fact that to achieve it, one has to pass through hard and difficult training, much more difficult than in many other kinds of GONG FU.

At first, leaps from a platform should be trained. For that purpose it is necessary to build a platform in the shape of a table, about two ZHANGs (about 6.6 m.) high. Dig a long and deep pit before the platform, fill it with sand to a depth of three CHIs (1 m.) approximately. Drive in a pile in each of four corners of the pit and tie a net made of thick cord to the piles at a height of about 2 CHIs (66 cm.) from sand surface. You need the net to fall on them after a leap to avoid injuring yourself. The trainee stands at the edge of the platform at attention, squats and raises his arms up at the same time, pushes off with his legs with force and leaps forward: his arms and all parts of the body are straightened and in horizontal plane.

After successful acquirement of leaping techniques from a platform one may proceed to exercise leaps above a plank. For that purpose, it is necessary to put a plank between two poles, the plank must be at a height of about 3 CHIs (1 m.) from the ground. There should be a pit with sand and a net immediately after the plank, the other is the same as above. The trainee stays at the platform at a distance of 2 or 3 ZHANGs (6.6 – 10 m.) from the plank, quickly runs to it, pushes off with two legs with force, his whole body stretches forward, like high jumps are made at the present time (probably, the author means pole vaults just at the moment of overcoming the plank) and flies over the plank. It is necessary to achieve in the process of training that the body should fly over the plank strictly in horizontal position. After that, change the plank with a board, 1,5 to 3 CHIs (0.5 – 1 m.) wide. The plank itself is very narrow and it is comparatively easy to overcome it. But to fly over a board, three CHIs wide, one should have certain knacks. Then, it is necessary to put the board on a wooden frame that is like a ring with daggers for acrobats. It is necessary to fly through the

frame. Increase gradually the number of frames to 6 or 7, one by one. Your success will be significant if you can freely fly through all the frames without touching them. At the next stage sharp knives should be installed at the edges of the frames (we strongly recommend not to do so), as a result of it the inner space of the frames decreases and the task will be much more complicated. If you can, even in this case, freely fly through the frames, it means that GONG FU "Piercing curtain" has been acquired to perfection. In that case, if the opening passes your body, you can freely "enter" and "leave". However, it is necessary to train yourself for 5 years at least, may be even for 8 to 10 years.

35. The Force of Eagle's Claws (YING ZHAO LI)

Another name of the exercise "The Force of Eagle's Claws" is "The Skill of Dragon's Claws" – LONG ZHAO GONG. That is nothing else but the skill of grips. The user of this method can cause unbearable pain to his enemy by gripping him with a hand. The method is a combination of the "soft" and "hard" GONG FU, hardness and flexibility, a union of YIN and YANG.

The training method is as follows: prepare a small jug weighing about 5 kg, clasp its neck on the outer side in a hand (with all five fingers) and raise it. At first, it will be somewhat inconvenient, but in a few months you will freely raise and lower it many times in succession. When you attain this, start to add a cup of grain into the jug each week until it is filled. Then replace grain with iron shots. Still later replace iron shots with pieces of iron. When you can raise and lower the jug filled with pieces of iron without particular effort, it will mean that training of the "hard" GONG FU and the "tough" YANG of "The Force of Eagle's Claws" is over. After that, training without jug is needed.

Training of the "softness" YIN of the skill "The Force of Eagle's Claws". Spread apart five fingers in the morning, point your arm toward the sun and make "gripping" and "pulling" movements, it is necessary to fill the arm with QI by will-power and concentrate force (in the arm) at that. When you attain this, it will mean that the "soft" GONG FU of "flexible" YIN "The

Force of Eagle's Claws" has been mastered. When you take a thing in a hand, some force is applied, that is the "hard" GONG FU belonging to the category YANG. When nothing is in your hands, force is not applied, it is the "soft" GONG FU belonging to the category YIN. Mutual coordination of YIN and YANG accounts for the training procedure: at first YANG, then YIN. "Hardness" and "Softness" are used at the same time, therefore training of "softness" supplements training of "hardness".

By training, such a level of mastership can be achieved that if, for example a bird is flying by and you stretch out your hand and make a prehensile movement, the bird falls down as if killed by an arrow. One more example: a horse stands at an distance of a few ZHANGs[61] from you and you make an arm movement as if you wish to lead it away, it will follow you as if you have reins in your hand. The same happens with people. If the "softness" YIN is not trained to perfection and only YANG has been mastered to the highest point of mastership, you can also inflict an injury to your enemy which is not precarious to his life. However, if you stop training half-way, you can get finger crookedness and that illness is not curable. Yang Bang Hou, the uncle of the prominent Pekinese specialist in TAYJI QUAN Yang Cheng Fu, had the use of this GONG FU to perfection. He could make a flying-by bird to perch on his hand: the bird flaps with its wings, but can not fly up.

Editor's notes:

[61] 1 ZHANG = 3.3 m.

In my time I also trained the skill "The Force of Eagle's Claws" and I freely raised a jug filled with iron shots. But during battles near Nankou in which I happened to participate I was wounded in the right leg. During a few months I underwent treatment, of course, I had to discontinue training. Unfortunately, until now all my fingers of both hands are crooked (see the photo).

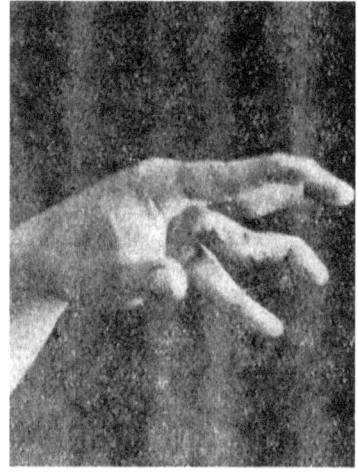

36. Technique "Iron Bull" (TIE NIU GONG)

You must not start to speak if you cannot answer for your words in future, and nobody has the right to say thoughtlessly everything at his own sweet will. If you wish to acquire a skill, learn to command your speech at first.

At the first stage the exercise "Iron Bull" is aimed at strengthening the external power of the body. It allows to develop the force YANG in the body. Deeper penetration into this skill learns to determine when to speak and when to keep silence[62]. As far as the use and efficiency are concerned, the technique is similar to that one of "Fabric Bag" (BU DAI GONG). This skill allows to repulse enemies, however crafty and skillful they are, with the use of all the power of the force YANG in the body for that purpose.

The method of acquiring the skill is as follows: first, it is necessary to concentrate the energy QI[63] in your stomach, then make circular movements on the stomach with your fingers. In

---

Editor's notes:

[62]"To open the mouth" (KAI KOU) and "To shut the mouth" (BI KOU) in the original text.
[63] A variant is "to fill the stomach with QI".

the beginning those movement should made without application of great force and almost without pressing the stomach. It is expedient to repeat this exercise several times a day and even during a rest. Then, the stomach should be rubbed[64] with a palm with the application of force. The stomach muscles and the skin will gradually become stronger.

After the acquirement of this part proceed to more complicated elements. It is necessary to punch repeatedly on the stomach now. It should be done several times a day. During first lessons you will feel dull pain that will disappear with time. Then, the force put into your blows must be gradually increased. You should strike not at a particular point but on the whole surface of the stomach.

After you learn to bear punches, proceed to the use of a wooden hammer and replace the wooden hammer with a iron hammer when blows with the wooden hammer do not cause painful feeling. When you just start to train blows with an iron hammer on the stomach, a dull sound will be heard as if you strike at a tree. If you are on the right way, that is you train correctly, the sound will gradually become more resonant, at the final stage it should be like a metal clang. It takes seven or eight months to acquire the skill.

Then, when your stomach gets used to the pressure of a metal object, proceed to training with a slab of stone weighing 180

Editor's notes:

[64] "To scrape" in the original text.

JINs (about 90 kg). Lie down on your back and put the slab on your stomach. With time you will be able to have a quiet and sound sleep (with the slab on your stomach) and will not feel any discomfort.

If you use each spare minute to train the technique "Iron Bull", your stomach will become excellent. Neither punches nor chopping blows of the enemy will be able to harm it. If the stomach is piked or slashed with a sharp knife, no single scratch will be on it. You will be sure that you will have no enemies. Those who speak a lot or those who keep silence for a long time can not be social, nothing to say about their ability to listen. But even such men, if they spend their time for training and exert efforts, will be able to acquire the technique of "Iron Bull". After the acquirement of the skill they can withstand even blows delivered by the Immortals.

37. Skill of Eagle Wings (YING YI GONG)

If you train yourself hard, you can crush even a stone.

The exercise "Skill of Eagle Wings" is aimed at strengthening the outer by exerting great efforts and nursing the force YANG in the body. The technique allows to develop the force of arms, strengthen elbows and joints, increase the force of fist and palm blows. If you acquire the technique, you will be able to beat off blows delivered by enemies both from close and far distance, with blunt and sharp, short and long weapons. If you wield the skill of "Eagle

Wings", you will be able to repel any attacks of enemies against you, whatever swiftly they will act.

The method for learning that skill is as follows. Dig two straight vertical wooden poles into the ground and fix a horizontal bar

above. Tie tightly two pieces of cord[65] to the horizontal bar and let their free ends hang down. Tie a bag with sand to each of those two cords. The bags must be at a height of about three and a half CHIs above the ground[66]. The distance between the bags must be about two CHIs[67], the bags can freely dangle in any direction.

As regard to the length of cords and the distance between bags the following can be additionally said. Suspended bags must be at the head level of the trainee. If the trainee takes the position MA BU[68] ("RIDER"), the bags (their upper part) must be at the head level approximately and the lower part (of bags) a bit lower than the shoulder line, but not lower than 6 or 7 CUNs[69]. In other words, the bags must have a size ensuring their upper part[70] to be at the ear level of the trainee who has assumed the position MA BU. All those who practise the exercise must give due attention to all those recommendations.

Editor's notes:

[65] "A draw-well cord" in the original text. Thus, the meaning is quite a strong cord capable of bearing a significant load.
[66] CHI, a Chinese measure of length approximately equal to one third of a meter, that is about 30 cm, in the metric system. Thus, the suspended bags should be at a level of one meter above the ground.
[67] 60 cm.
[68] The position MA BU is denoted as "QIMA BU" in the original text.
[69] CUN, a Chinese traditional measure of length equal to 1/30 meter, that is the bags should not be lower than 20 cm from the shoulder line of the trainee.
[70] That is the one to which a cord is tied.

As regard to the weight, the following can be said: at the first stages of training the weight of each bag must be 10 JINs[71].

The training method is as follows. The trainee stands between the bags, fixes his body in the position MA BU, bends his arms in elbows, and places them at shoulder level so that each of his clenched fists should be opposite the half of the chest to which it corresponds and face each other. The elbows should be turned so that arms (shoulders and forearms) with their outer parts (surfaces) point upward and touch the suspended bags with sand in such a manner that they can be lifted with the use of bent arms. Pressure caused by the weight of sand bags must be brought to arms, not to the cord. When you exhaust, you can break your training for a while to return later to the exercise.

The exercise should be trained once a day, each morning. It is necessary to do it 30 times during each training, gradually increasing training time (i.e. the time of continuously holding bags hanging), and number of repetitions. By the end of one-year training number of repetitions must reach 100 times. Each month in the course of the year the weight of a bag should be increased by 2 JINs[72]. Thus, by the end of one-year training the weight of each bag should be 34 JINs[73]. By the end of the first training year the force which allows to hold heavy things by hanging is evident.

Editor's notes:

[71] JIN, a Chinese traditional measure of weight equal to half a kilogram. Thus, the weight of a bag will be equal to 5 kg.
[72] That is by 1 kg.
[73] That corresponds to 17 kg.

After acquiring the above-described, one can proceed to the next training stage. At first, it is necessary to use bags with sand weighing 20 JINs[74] hung on a cord as before. The trainee concentrates, sits in the stance MA BU, bends his arms in elbows and tightly press them to the sides. Then he sets his elbows aside and raises them up with force, the movement should be made with "ejection" of force. It is necessary to touch the lower part of suspended bags with elbow joints and push them up. In the beginning the bags will fly up 1 or 2 CUNs[75], not higher. However, with higher level of training the height at which the bags will fly up because of a blow will gradually increase. Finally, you will be able to throw up a bag with an elbow blow to a height of two CHIs[76] or even more. It is necessary to add 5 JINs of weight[77] to a suspended bag each time. It should be done each time before you start training to make it more effective. Five JINs of weight should be added until the weight of a bag reaches 50 JINs[78]. In that case it can be asserted that you have reached great mastership.

Having perfected in the skill of "Eagle Wings", the man can use all possibilities of his body to push away enemy to three ZHANGs[79]. To acquire this skill is as simple as to tear a sheet of paper. The efficiency of the method is tremendous. You can

---

Editor's notes:

[74] 10 kg.
[75] About 3.3-6.6 cm.
[76] 60 cm.
[77] 2.5 kg.
[78] 25 kg.
[79] ZHANG is a Chinese traditional measure of length equal to 3.33 m. Thus, 3 ZHANGs are equal to 10 m approximately.

beat off enemy' spears with your elbows, deliver blows of huge force at enemies, use "deadly arm" (SHA SHOW)[80] more effectively, and stop (falling, rolling) stones. If you go on training this technique for a long time, your arms and elbows will become stronger. Learning the technique is also beneficial for your lungs.

Editor's notes:

[80] SHA SHOU, under that name are grouped several exercises out of "72 Arts" aimed at training arms, fists, fingers, and palms to deliver blows of great destructive force.

38. Hand of Sun Rays (YANG GUANG SHOU)

The skill of "The Arm of Sun Rays" is a soft GONG FU, it develops the internal power and belongs to the YIN category. It is somewhat easier to obtain mastership in this GONG FU than in such skills as "One finger of meditation Chan" (see par.#7) and "Cinnabar Palm" (see par.#17), and so there are many known masters in this kind of

WU SHU (Martial Arts). One of them, my acquaintance, lives in the province of Liaoning. He is Guo Li Zheng, a master in SHAOLIN QUAN, already over seventy. He is a stone-deaf Taoist who acquired this kind of GONG FU during three years. Once I witnessed such a scene: he pointed the hand at a dog at some distance from it and it began to bark at once. Another man (I don't want to disclose his name and surname) learnt XING YI QUAN (HSING YI CHUAN) at first, then became a disciple of GUO and perfected his Shaolin WU SHU. At that time master Guo was the head of the society for learning WU SHU in the town of Shenyang. A quarrel happened between the tutor and his disciple because of some or another insignificant reason. The disciple even allowed himself to insult his tutor. Guo unconsciously moved a fist toward his disciple. In the beginning the disciple did not feel anything, but in an hour pain spread over his whole back. That is just, as they say, "to hit the cow over a mountain", it is often mentioned in novels about knights.

The method of training is very simple: it is necessary to take an oil lamp or a candle and burn it. The height of flame must be about 0.5 CUN (about 1.5 cm). Put the lamp (or the candle) on a table, stand before the lamp at a distance of 3 CHIs (1 m), assume the stance "Rider", concentrate QI in the lower part of your stomach, concentrate your attention and punch toward the flame at some distance from it. Go on with training until an aromatic candle burns down. It is necessary to train yourself in the morning and in the evening without breaking for a single day. If the flame extinguishes from punching at that distance (three CHIs), the first result has been obtained. After that, go away from the table at a distance of 8 steps. If one punch can extinguish the flame, it is the full success. If you punch a man at a distance of two or three steps without touching his body, that man will feel sharp pain. Specialists think that QI which is set to motion by a fist belongs to the YIN category, therefore it is difficult to oppose to such a punch with anything.

39. Exercise for Groin (MEN DAN GONG)

This kind of GONG FU is also called "Skill of a Golden Cicada" (JIN CHAN GONG). It is the "soft" GONG FU that trains the "outer" power and it belongs to the YIN category. It is a very difficult method. It makes the scrotum as hard as stone and iron.

The training method is as follows. It is necessary to quietly sit cross-legged, put out from one's head all extraneous thoughts, discard all anxiety, have the pure and open heart. It is necessary to mobilize QI in the whole body and concentrate it in the lower part of the stomach below the navel, then direct QI up on the spine and let it reach the brain and then lower it down along the front part of the body to DANTIAN. Thus, QI makes a circle in the body. It must be done several times daily, but do not try to speed it up. Otherwise, you will get tired physically and morally without any use. In the beginning you will have no any special feeling, but with time, when you learn to concentrate QI in the lower part of your stomach, the scrotum and the penis will become harder, it means that the first stage of training is over.

After that, it is necessary to sit quietly with your crossed legs and tap on testicles with a palm. It is quite painful in the beginning. However, it is necessary to concentrate QI and go on training. Painful felling will disappear in the course of time. It means that the second stage of training is over. After that it is necessary to stand up straightly and punch with great force. If

even in that case no painful feeling appears, it means the final aim has been reached. In the process of training it is necessary to refrain from sexual life and to discard even a thought about it.

40. Exercise "Iron Bag" (TIE DAI GONG)

The exercise "Iron Bag" is the "hard" GONG FU, it develops the outer power and belongs to the category YANG. That method develops the ability to "eject force" (FA LI). It is necessary to train yourself in a pair. But at first, it is necessary to stitch a square bag out of several layers of thick fabric and fill it with iron shot. The weight of the smallest bag must be about 5 kg and the weight of the biggest one 20 to 25 kg. It will depend on the strength and physical development of trainees. The bag can be replaced with a heavier one with time.

During a training, two men stand side by side at a distance of 3 ZHANGs (about 10 m). One man takes the bag at its middle part with his right hand, lifts it to the shoulder level and throws toward the second man. The second man sees the bag fly toward him, sees it just before his eyes now, is ready to raise his hands and catch the bag, but it is better to shift a little bit aside, let the bag pass and reach the left shoulder and at that moment catch the rear part of the bag with right hand (i.e. the right hand catches the flying bag after it has passed you). It is necessary to catch the bag for its middle part, either, and stand firmly and steady. If you catch the bag for its angle or its edge, the training will lack efficiency. A flying bag has great cinematic energy and it is quite difficult to catch for its middle part after it has passed, but it is necessary to do as one should do and not as one wishes to do. After accepting the bag, throw it back without any delay. Throw the bag to each other in such a manner several dozens. Then, change hands and throw and catch with your left hand. It

is desirable that the trainees would be of the same height and physical strength. Otherwise, serious disadvantages will occur: if the height of the partners is different, the trajectory of the bag will deviate from the horizontal one, and if the partners are of different physical strength, the bag flies at different speeds, it will be difficult for a weaker man to catch it. If he still manages to catch the bag with difficulty, the jerk will be too strong and he may loose his balance and, moreover, get injured.

Too heavy bag should not be used at the first stage. For example, if you can quite easily carry with an arm a bag filled with iron shot and weighing 10 kg by holding at its middle part, you should train yourself with a bag weighing not more than 5 kg. First, it needs much more strength for training with a flying bag than for simply carrying a bag of the same weight, second, it is necessary to observe the principle of succession. Unstitch the bag after three months of training, add 0.5 or 1 kg of shot and go on training. Add the same amount after another three months. Continue to gradually add shot until the weight of the bag increases up to 25-30 kg. It will take 4 or 5 years from the beginning to the end. After the acquirement of this GONG FU, if you happen to meet even a strong and heavy enemy, you will be able to lift him and throw at a distance of several ZHANGs[81]: thanks to the exercise, you know, there exists a huge power of a jerk which is difficult to oppose to.

Editor's notes:

[81] 1 ZHANG = 3.3 m.

While training, it is necessary to pay attention to the following points:

1. A bag thrown must fly strictly on the horizontal line.

2. The man who catches a flying bag must let it pass in front of him, then catch it for its middle part from behind (as if in pursuit of it). You should not fling your arm toward the bag, don't catch it for its angles and edges. It is associated with the following facts: if you catch an incoming bag, you can injure your fingers and wrists, and if you catch for bag edges, training will be inefficient.

3. In whatever posture you stand, your feet must stand firmly. If the position of the man who throws is unstable, the force of a throw decreases. If the feet of the man who accepts the bag do not stand firmly, his body will lose its balance and it will lead not to success but to an injury.

The above three points are very important. As to a bigger weight of a bag and a distance between the trainees, it is better to take into consideration your own possibilities instead of adhering to old requirements.

41. Method that Reveals the Truth (JIE DI GONG)

*Those who learn martial arts often
need help and support.*

JIE DI GONG is designed to give hardness to the outer parameters of the body and rear the force YANG in the body, it also allows to consolidate the energy QI inside a human body. The method of learning this art entails great difficulties. It will be very hard for the trainee at initial stages, the probability for the internal organs to be damaged is very high and it is hardly to avoid damages. When learning the skill, one must not proceed quickly from one stage to another[82].

Those who learn the JIE DI GONG skill must acquire the so-called technique of "Eighteen somersaults" (DI SHIBA GUN) and the technique of falling on the ground (DI TANG GONG FU)[83] to perfection. Besides the above mentioned, the trainees must also acquire other methods of falls and jumps, for instance, such as the somersault JIAN HU JI SHI[84]. Those

---

Editor's notes:

[82] Hieroglyph CUAN that literally means "jumping from one to another" stands in the original text.
[83] DI TANG GONG FU can be also translated as "To obtain mastery of the skill through tumbling on the ground".
[84] This expression can be translated as "martial art of crossing rivers and lakes" (in the original text: "JIANG" is a river, "HU" is a lake, "JI" is a technique, and "SHI" is a warrior).

methods can be grouped into: forward somersaults, backward somersaults, leftward somersaults, rightward somersaults, and others. Among them are "arrow somersault"[85] (JIAN PAN), "fall on the back" (BEI DIE), "running jump and somersault" (ZHI DIE), "fall with the face up" (YANG DIE), "fall prone" (FU DIE) and other methods.

It is necessary to start learning this skill from acquiring forward somersaults. Move the right arm to the left side, lean the right shoulder and the head on the ground carefully, turn the body so that the waist is raised a little. That is the method of a straight somersault over the right shoulder. The method of a straight somersault over the left shoulder is as follows: it is necessary to touch the right side with your left hand, lean the left shoulder and the head on the ground carefully, and turn the body so that the waist region is raised a little.

The second form of falling which should be acquired by the learners additionally includes a forward running jump and it is the easiest for learning. As a matter of fact, that is a forward somersault. The head is pointed forward at that, the body turns so that the waist region is raised a little. The movement resembles the somersault FAN JIN DOU and looks, to a great degree, like a cat that is tumbling.

There is also a backward somersault which is done from the back over the head and is called a "reverse somersault". There is

---

Editor's notes:

[85] Here and further is literal translation of terms.

also a leftward somersault which is executed as follows: the left shoulder leans on the ground and a left turn of the body is done over the head. A rightward somersault is executed in the similar way when the body turns to the right from the right shoulder over the head.

After acquiring rightward and leftward somersaults that are not the most complicated elements in JIE DI GONG but allow to create the base for learning exercises to be followed, one should proceed to learn methods of falling back. The body in those exercises must purposefully fall backward. At first, the back should turn a little to the right, that is to move the right shoulder forward, the left arm should be placed back and to the left, it should rest on the ground. The body should turn to the left and tilt. It is necessary to fall down from above on the left arm. Then, applying some force, set one hand on the ground and make the body take a vertical position (with the head down), do a somersault after it and stand up. This exercise is called "The wheel that rolls on a flat surface" – PING DI FAN CHE.

The skill of straight fall back ZHI DIE FA is as follows. The trainee squats so that his back in that position is straight and falls backward on the back. When he starts to tilt back, in the beginning he has to move one arm back and rest it on the ground, when his body reaches the surface, he has to make a somersault with a support on that arm, shift the body weight to it, push off from the ground with that arm with force and stand up. The exercise can and must be done both for the left and right arm.

The so-called "Carp's somersault" LIYU DA TING, also known as "fall with the face up" (YANG DIE), is made from a standing position. It is necessary to tilt (bend in the waist) back so that the face should be pointed up. When the body is tilting back, the head should tilt a little forward, that is toward the chest. Do not fall on the ground at any account: at the moment when the body is tilting back, it is necessary to lift left and right arm and stretch them toward the ground. After reaching the surface of the ground (with hands), it is necessary to do an overturn with a support on the arms, push off the surface and stand up.

The so-called "Technique of iron bridge" (TIE BAN QIAO) which we also know under the name "fall prone" (FU DIE) includes the following. It is necessary to fall forward prone from a position of standing on straight legs. While falling, the body should be absolutely straight, it is forbidden to bend legs in knees. When the body approaches the ground, it is necessary to bend arms in elbows and clench fists. In a fall, it is necessary to land neither on the chest nor on the stomach, but on bent arms and fists. Then, it is necessary to push off from the ground with arms and take the standing position.

The last of the somersaulting methods is called PU HU SHI[86]. It is quite difficult to execute it. It is necessary to bend in the waist and bend the arms in elbows, rest with both arms on the floor,

---

Editor's notes:

[86] Here "PU" means "to push, to dash, to rush"; "HU" means a tiger, "SHI" means a form.

the head and shoulders being also pressed to the surface. The legs are turned over to the top and make a rotating movement, the body is lying in the vertical plane, a somersault is done from that position.

At first those exercises will be done relatively slowly and they can hurt. The trainee will do somersaults deftly and swiftly over time and he will be able to acquire the skill of "eighteen somersaults" at an eyewink. Besides "Eighteen somersaults", JIE DI GONG includes 64 other kinds. If you earnestly learn the above techniques from the start, the way to success will not be easy. Those who started to acquire somersaults since early childhood and made great efforts to reach perfection in that skill spent a lot of time to learn and master JIE DI GONG. Great masters who have mastered JIE DI GONG to perfection can do uncountable number of somersaults rightward and leftward, forward and backward, standing up and falling again and again, that's why their QI becomes fresher with every day. Those exercises result in skin, bones, and muscles to become stronger.

There are no such tutors at our time who could properly pass down secrets of that skill to the mob. It is necessary to consolidate the Spirit in the hearts of disciples and through it develop their mastership. Recommendations can be given, but secrets of a skill can not be passed down by means of words. If you don't make progress in techniques of falling on the ground, you will not reach full perfection in all other kinds of the skill.

42. Skill of Tortoise Back (GUI BEI GONG)

One should not concentrate too much on the sense.

"The Skill of Tortoise Back" is aimed at strengthening the outer power of the body and rearing the power YANG. This skill serves for training the back to strengthen it. Its effectiveness is not inferior to that one of techniques for strengthening and training the stomach, such as the "Skill of Fabric Bag" (BU DAI GONG; par.#69) and the "Skill of Iron Stomach" (TIE DAI

GONG; par.#36). That technique is very effective and allows to withstand blows of enemies.

Mainly bones are in the upper part of the back, therefore it is relatively easy to train this section. On the contrary, it is extremely difficult to train and strengthen the lower part where the kidneys surrounded with soft parts are situated. Those who seriously practise "The skill of tortoise back" must pay special

attention to those sections where important internal organs are situated[87]. Devotees of GUI BEI GONG must train the part of their body which goes from the head and the neck to the region of the coccyx. So, it is necessary to lay stress on strengthening the whole surface of the back.

At first, before strengthening the soft parts of the back, special attention should be paid to the development of QI. The development of QI starts from massage of the waist with hands (palms). Every day before getting up and going to bed, one should sit in the posture of meditation[88], close the eyes and empty consciousness, concentrate on rearing QI. Then, it is necessary to press on the back of the waist with both hands. At first, it is necessary to rub the back toward inside 36 times and, then do the same toward outside. That exercise should be done one time. After it being done, it is necessary to arrange fingers so that the forefinger and the middle finger should touch the pad of the thumb with their pads and joints between the second and third phalanges (of the forefinger and the middle finger) be bent and protruded. The protruded joints should press on the soft parts of the back with circular movements. Both hands should move simultaneously. Each hand must do 360 presses (circular movements).

Editor's notes:

[87] "Soft places" in the original text.
[88] "In the posture of contemplation" in the original text.

That exercise being acquired, it is necessary to add one more training cycle and then another one so that total number of cycles should be three. When you are doing the exercise, you should thoroughly count each movement and keep in mind their exact number. One must not make mistake at any account. If you make more or less movements than required, it can lead to illnesses or damages of the body. Moreover, counting movements beneficially influences the man, develops his memory and attention and allows to prevent from appearing any extraneous thoughts during a training process. While training, the man should not see the world around him, should not see anything but the tip of his nose, it is the same as if you look just at your own heart. The above-described exercises must be repeated two times each day. After one year the back and the kidneys will be sure to become extremely strong.

After that training cycle is over, one should proceed to training through blows. At first, a stick of soft wood are to be used as a mallet. At an initial stage even a cane or a reed stalk will suit. The cane should be clenched in fist. While doing the exercise, QI should be concentrated in the region of the back, especially in the region of the waist. It is necessary to beat at one's back so that no unbeaten place was left on the back. Beating should be done steadily at upper, lower, right, and left parts of the back. At first, while beating, do not apply force. It is necessary to increase the strength of blows gradually in the process of further training. Blows must be heavier over time.

You must learn some special aspects of the technique of "Iron Back" during the time between training. It will allow to increase

the applied force and link together training of upper, lower, and middle parts of the back. The Chinese in the South strenuously train the whole back. They do it in the following way. A cord is wound around the chest and the shoulders, the man lies on some hard (inclined) board with his face up and moves down on it. It helps not only to strengthen the back, but allows to successfully withstand heavy blows as well.

The technique of "Iron Back" is considered to be quite difficult. The strength of blows in it should be gradually increased too. At first, a stick of soft wood is also used, then you proceed to training with an iron rod. Finally, you proceed to an iron hammer through gradual complication of training. Proceed with time to a heavier iron hammer which allows a man to make more sensitive and much heavier blows compared with stick or rod blows. Naturally, at first, training will cause some painful sensations, but the acquirement of the true skill impossible without them.

When you acquire that skill, any blows delivered by your enemies will not leave even a scratch on your back. You will not notice even an ax blow. While making movements, some disciples introduce to them the Consciousness instead of the Spirit, force the Spirit with a thought, direct QI and concentrate it in the region between shoulders, kidneys, and waist. Then, when they happen to receive blows helter-skelter on the back, their Spirit and QI will be in disorderly (chaotic, unstable) state

and it will be difficult for them to concentrate even if they wish to do that very much[89].

It is the best way to learn "The Skill of Tortoise Back" at the same time with the technique of "Iron Head" (TIE TOU GONG; par.#8), the technique of "Iron Shirt" (TIE BU SHAN; par.#9) and the technique of "Iron Stomach" (TIE DAI GONG; #36). It might be matched with breath training as well, which is very useful for training self-control and fortitude. Only after learning all that, you may be said to have acquired mastery in full measure.

The whole body becomes strong as a metal. Besides, the trainees will be able to easily proceed to learning the skills "Cinnabar Palm" (ZHU SHA ZHANG; par.#17) and "Fist YIN" (YIN QUAN; par.#64) as well as other "soft" techniques from the YIN section. It should be learnt nothing else at the same time. Too quick transition to new things (without consolidating the previous material) will be fraught with various body damages which can be caused by enemies. At first, one

---

Editor's notes:

[89] Please pay attention to the epigraph before that exercise: "One should not concentrate too much on the sense". If you learn to direct QI into a certain part of the body with an effort of consciousness (thought), you will be able to make it (just that part) invulnerable only during the time when you consciously concentrate on it. However, that ability is suitable only for demonstration on a circus ring. You can not foresee in an actual combat where the enemy will deliver a blow (or a series of blows), therefore such a "skill" will be of small benefit. The purpose of the Shaolin "hard", or "fighting" QI GONG is to fill the whole body with the internal energy QI and make it invulnerable. Accordingly, while training, the Spirit and the Consciousness must not be artificially concentrated in some separate part of the body.

should acquire niceties better. Learning the "internal" techniques of the Shaolin Art is impossible without acquirement of Wudan[90] training techniques of QI.

Editor's notes:

[90] It means mountains of Wudan in the province of Hubei where one the Taoist centers in China, the birth-place of the so-called "Wudan" school of Martial Arts, is situated.

43. Skill of Deft Jumps (CUAN ZONG SHU)

Only hard work leads to constancy in mastery.

"Skill of jumps" is a soft GONG FU, it leads to strengthening the internal. The way to the acquirement of that skill is also soft. In the past knights devoted their whole life to the acquirement of the skill. Now, when science thrives and develops, there are no outstanding achievements in that field. People show irresponsibility toward repetition of what they have studied and toward training. It is horrible to see that a good half of the people take the road of crime and cruelty. The reason is that spirituality which fed the Middle Empire and the Chinese nation in the past and feeds in the present gradually disappears and is doomed to obscurity. Cultured and educated people dip their brushes into ink-pots and jabber as before, they do not answer for their own words. One can feel sincerely sorry for them: they failed to properly succeed in civil branches of sciences, not to mention their achievements in military ones. All comes to proclamation of truths to the mob by the people who have high opinion of themselves as Teachers. But has all this idle talk anything to do with the true Martial Art?

In the recent past some official Han from the province of Shandong narrated about a man called Guang Zhi Fei who could walk on walls and cornices. But nobody thought Han's story to be true. Indeed, a good half of people in the past thought that tales about "Skill of jumps" were ridiculous chatter, not worth of trusting. That happened because few people who

acquired that skill to perfection hid and kept his mastery in secret.

The method of the acquirement of "Skill of jumps" can not be discussed without mentioning obligatory use of lead in the training process[91]. Due to effect of lead, blisters and internal bruises may appear on the skin, they can cause the formation of abscesses in future. To avoid that, lead must be heated on fire until it becomes red and then dip it into pig's blood. Before that, it is necessary to dip lead into a vessel filled with pig's blood and leave it there for one night and only after that lead should be heated on fire and dipped into pig's blood as above described. Repeat (heating and soaking in pig's blood) seven times. After pig's blood interacts with lead, the color of lead will become dark-violet, such lead is called "dead" lead. The lead treated so should be dug into earth for 49 days for full elimination of its poisonous properties. After lead is dug out, it must be washed in clean water. After that lead is ready for use.

The way to use the obtained substance is as follows. Lead is placed into narrow canvas bags which are wrapped around calves and forearms. Such bag can be also fixed along the backbone. The bags can be of different mass but the weight of each bag should not exceed 8 JINs (4 kg). Learning "Skill of jumps" should start from running on mountain roads and passes. It is the foundation for the acquirement of the

---

Editor's notes:

[91] It is a matter of the use of small lead pieces as a filler for bags that are fixed on legs and arms for doing the exercise (see below).

technique. Each day, after "wrapping with lead", it is necessary to run on mountain roads and passes very fast. One year later, after a solid foundation is laid, you may proceed to learn running on the edge of a vat (PAO GANG GONG FU). That technique implies that the trainee must go on the upper edge of a big vat[92]. At the same time running on standing stone piles (YI ZU PAO LI ZHUAN) can be acquired. Long stone piles standing on the ground are used for that purpose. It is necessary to move on the top from one pile to another. The purport of the exercise is not to dump the piles while running on them . It is the first half of "Skill of jumps".

The second part in the acquirement of that skill is as follows. It is necessary to stand erect with legs unbent in knees and the back unbent in the waist. It is necessary to jump up, using the force of arms and legs and planting the feet (on the ground). You should train yourself in such a way until you can jump up at a height of one CHI (33 cm). Untie the bags with lead then, squat and jump up. One can exceed a height of two ZHANGs (6.6 m) in such a jump.

After that aspect of "Skill of jumps" being acquired, proceed to jumps out of a pit. The pit should be 4-5 CHIs (1.30 to 1.70 m) wide and its depth should gradually increase from one to two ZHANGs (from 3.3 m to 6.6 m). It is necessary to jump out of the pit as high as possible. Squat on the bottom of the pit, push off with legs and jump up, using the force of elasticity available

---

Editor's notes:

[92] See details concerning it in paragraph #44 "Skill of Light Body".

in your knees. The body will move in the air. It is necessary to fling your arms forward and up in the beginning of a jump and lower them forward and down at the final phase. Thus, the whole force of the body will be directed upward. At the moment when the trainee can jump out the pit fully and touch the ground with his toes, it will mean that he is in full command of "Skill of jumps".

Seven or eight years of hard training can not be thought a perfect mastery. Regular exercises and continuous improvement of the technique are required. When the trainee acquires the technique to full extent, his body will become light and will be able to move at a significant speed. He will be able to move much faster than any other man. He will be able to ascend and descend at a great speed, jump high and overcome high obstacles. He will be able to move on wall of a room and move as if he flies. "Skill of jumps" is absolutely noiseless, therefore it can be used even at nights. The skill being studied completely, it can be used against bandits and offenders.

So-called "Skill of jumps", it is also called "The skill of walking on cornices and walls", as well as jumps over houses and other similar techniques are thought to be absurd. At our time "The skill of jumps" is kept up by some family dynasties and passed over from father to son, but it gradually "goes out of fashion". Few people can bear 6 or 7 years of hard training and feel no doubt in efficiency of that skill even for a second.

44. Skill of Light Body (JIN SHEN SHU)

Only tenacious work leads to constancy.

"The skill of light body" is a soft way to strengthen the internal. It is not simple to acquire the skill of "Light body". Thanks to the knowledge of the skill even the people whose bodies weigh over 100 JINS[93] can easily take a rest on the branch of a tree like a butterfly or a bee. It is not complicated for them to fly like a swallow but it is not easy and quick way to achieve such a result.

At the first stage the training method of "The skill of light body" is similar to that one employed when learning "The skill of deft jumps" (CUAN ZONG SHU)[94] and "The skill of movement in the air" (FEI XING GONG)[95]. At the first training stage a big vat filled with water and put on seven stones is used. The trainees move on the edge the vat, execute different techniques, deliver blows etc. PAO GANG BIEN, "running on edge of a vat", that is called. While doing that exercise, the trainee carries on his back a canvas bag filled with iron chips or lead soaked with pig blood. The weight of the bag is 1 JIN (0.5 kg).

Editor's notes:

[93] **50 kg.**
[94] **See details in par.#43.**
[95] **See details in par.#53.**

It is necessary to take out one calabash-sized dipper of water from the vat at the middle of each month or on the 21-st day of each month and add one or two pieces of lead or iron into the bag filled with lead or iron chips which the trainee carries on his back. After that the trainee continues to train himself as above. It is necessary to scoop out one more dipper of water from the vat one month later and add a little lead or metal chips into the bag. One shall stop only after no water is left in the vat and weight of lead or metal chips in the bag reaches 5 JINs (2.5 kg).

When the trainee can move on the edge of the empty vat without overturning it, he may proceed to improve himself in that exercise on a big basket filled with small iron pieces. The principle of movement on the edge of the basket does not differ from that one on the edge of a vat and the amount of iron pieces in the basket should be decreased until the basket is empty. When the trainee acquires the movement on the edge of the empty basket, he may be said to have reached a lot.

Now the trainee may proceed to the next training stage. It is necessary to scatter coarse sand in a thin layer to form a path. The width of the path should not exceed 1 CHI (33 cm). Sand is covered with sheets of thin paper on which the trainee in "The skill of light body" will move. At first footprints of the trainee will be seen distinctly, but over time he will leave almost no prints. The paper sheet by sheet is gradually removed and the trainee starts to train himself in walking on the sand without making marks on it and without leaving no footprints.

Learning of that skill is thought to be over only when steps of the trainee becomes so light that when he walks on the grass he will not trample it down and will not leave any marks even on newly-

fallen snow. He must do all that without taking a bag with iron chips or lead off his shoulders. In that case he will be able to walk on water without leaving circles or ripples on it.

If one practices that skill during less than 12 years, he does not obtain perfection in it. When a man reaches the lightness in his body which is inherent in Celestials, he will be able to move and stop at spots he likes. Those wonderful people who lived in the past could "fly" over grass, move on water and snow without leaving any traces behind them. Those were noble knights who had acquired "The skill of light body" as well as other aspects of mastery. Highly cultured men admired them and described them in their works of art, they had no a slightest idea how it was difficult to master that skill to perfection.

If somebody starts to learn that skill in his childhood, he will be able to learn to run on stone piles[96], on the edge of a vat or a basket within two years. By that time, that is two year after, the amount of small iron pieces in the basket decreases more than by a half. When the movement on the edge of a basket is acquired, you have to fall down from the basket on the flat surface, stand up erect and fall down again. And even in that case the body must not leave any marks on the sand.

Those who abandoned and stopped training after having met some difficulties tear their hair out from disappointment that

---

Editor's notes:

[96] That exercise belongs to "The skill of deft jumps" and it was describes in the previous para. #43.

they could not acquire that skill. There is a great deal of talk about that skill now, there is a demand for it; however, it is difficult to learn the skill as it was before.

45. Exercise "Iron Knees" (TIE XI GONG)

The first part of this exercise is superb, its final part incomparable.

The exercise "Iron knees" belongs to the "hard" and "external" section of GONG FU, it develops the YANG force. Its specialty is strengthening knees for use in a combat and it especially suits to those styles of the Pugilistic Art where knee butts are widely used. That's why that section is not obligatory for the most of people. But the people who learn Martial Arts should not avoid to learn diffcrent techniques and methods of body strengthening. The more they acquire techniques the better. We are speaking about each part of the body separately, but it is necessary to get unity through training for a long time[97]. As you know, a small part (of the body) can be also attacked. Sometimes common (simple) exercises will be of great use and they can help to subdue your enemy.

The training method of the exercise "Iron knees" is as follows. It is necessary to sit with knees bent and legs crossed, tightly clench both fists and punch at the kneecaps. After punching 72 times, unclench your fists and rub the knee joints with your

---

Editor's notes:

[97] It means here that all parts of the body without exception must be strengthened.

palms applying force in the direction from outside to inside, 36 times altogether, then in opposite direction from inside to outside, also 36 times altogether. Continue to punch after rubbing, the number of punches is as above. It is necessary to execute nine series of rubbing and punching and finish the exercise with that.

Every day, before getting up, it is necessary to do the exercise one time. After one-year training the knee joint becomes stronger and you may proceed to training with the use of wooden hammers. It is necessary to make a pair of fist-sized hammers, their shape resembles a drum or a pearl, it is of no importance. Wrap the handles of the hammers with thick willow twigs or reed. It must be done because that gives the combination of the "soft" and "hard" when soft willow twigs are wound on the hard stick. Deliver blows at the knees with both hammers simultaneously, rub as before after 72 blows and deliver blows again. Repeat nine times altogether and finish the exercise with that. Exercise in such a way during one year, as a result of that knee joints will strengthen and become harder. After it the wooden hammers may be replaced with iron ones. The size of the iron hammers is the same as the size of wooden ones, each hammer should weigh 1 to 1.5 JIN (0.5 to 0.75 kg). You have to train according the above method during one year and then, after regular training, the exercise "Iron knees" can be considered as finished successfully.

After the successful end of that last training stage both knees will be as if they are forged of iron. It will be possible to break any object and cause a serious damage to the enemy by knee butting. That skill gives an advantage over the enemy to those who have acquired it, the only thing required is to forestall him

and give him no chance to use arms or legs for delivering blows. Butting with knees can be successfully used not only in attack but in defense too. Combat methods provide for the use of knees together with other kinds of blows, but knee butting can be also used separately. Knees are used both for attacking and defending actions. But it is necessary to take into account that a bone occupies the bigger and muscles smaller part in the knee joint and knees are barely coated with skin. Therefore, knees of ordinary people are not strong enough and can be easily damaged, they can not be used to full power. That exercise should be trained during two years at least and only in that case a good result can be obtained. It is easy to acquire that exercise.

46. Technique of Jumps (TIAO YAO FA)

It is necessary to be persistent in doing a hard exercise.

Training jumps is a part of "soft" work which strengthens the "inner", it belongs to exercises of "easy body" (JIN SHEN GONG). It is also called "Skill of overjumping" (CHAO JU GONG). That exercise is a must for those who practise Martial Arts. One should well keep it in mind and strive to do that exercise often. If you need to step aside five steps for a run to overcome  an obstacle, plug up spirit and brace oneself[98], that is not the real skill yet. It is of no importance at all if it is a high wall or a steep slope or uneven ground with hillocks, it is possible to move along easily and freely without paying any attention to all those obstacles.

Editor's notes:

[98]Literally in the original text: " In order QI to drone like a drum".

At the first stage loads of iron or sand must be tightly bound around the body, but their weight should not be great. Dig out in the ground a pit, one CHI (0.33 m) deep, and with such a diameter that two men could freely stand in it. The trainee stands in the center of the pit and executes high jumps, trying to jump out of the pit at his own choosing. Do that exercise many times in succession. At first the pit is not deep and the loads with iron chips are light, it is quite simple to make jumps out of the pit. Then, it will be necessary to make the pit deeper so that you could not jump out of the pit but could go out of the pit by raising your leg. After that, deepen the pit by one CUN (3.33 cm) in each 10 days or half a month and increase the weight by one LIAN (0.05 kg). Deepen the pit gradually and increase the weight, trying to do jumps easily and freely.

As a result of it the depth of the pit will reach three CHIs (about 1 meter). It will be substantially more difficult to do the exercise now. Therefore, if you earlier deepened the pit with an interval of 10 days to half a month, now you have to increase the interval to half a month or 20 days. Continue to increase the weight and train yourself as before. Over time the pit will be 5 CHIs (about 1.7 m) deep. After that, it will be necessary to continue training and increase the depth of the pit from 5 to 7 CHIs (about 2.3 m) and from 7 CHIs to 1 ZHANG (3.3 m). When the depth of the pit reaches 1 ZHANG and the weight of the loads 5 or 7 JINs (2.5-3.5 kg) and jumping out of the pit is done easily and freely, the training has reached its aim. Take off the loads in that case and increase the depth of the pit to 2 ZHANGs (about 6.6 m), train yourself in jumping out of the pit until you can do it easily and freely. Please note that after you overcame the depth of one ZHANG with the loads, it is necessary to take off the loads and increase at once the depth of the pit as much as twice.

It is necessary to train oneself from 3 to 5 years at least in such a way. If you think that you are in a hopeless situation, don't despair: if in the past somebody reached a success, that means you will be able to do the same. Many people stopped half way under the pressure of some circumstances and under the influence of somebody's opinion, it's quite regrettable thing, indeed!

47. Palm of Iron Sand (TIE SHA ZHANG)

It is not easy to study medicine and understand effects of drugs.

The skill "Palm of Iron Sand" (TIE SHA ZHANG) that can be also found under the name of "Hand of Black Sand" (HEI SHA SHOW) serves for strengthening of the external power of the body and rearing the force YANG in it. To acquire that skill, it is necessary to employ special methods and means. Besides, special attention should be paid to training QI, which will undoubtedly promote the development and the internal improvement of the body.

We shall speak at first about a secret recipe for hand training. It is necessary to take 5 JINs (2.5 kg) of strong spirit, 10 JINs (5 kg) REN ZHONG BANG[99], and 10 JINs (5 kg) of white vinegar, mix it up and cook it to the state of thick soup. Then cool it and cook

---

Editor's notes:

[99] Febrifuge made of humane urine in Chinese traditional medicine.

again. Each cooking must be within the exact time needed for burning three aromatic sticks[100]. After cooking for the fourth time the thickness of the mixture becomes suitable for use. Then small iron grains (iron chips) should be added to the substance obtained. When doing this, the mixture should be mashed with a wooden dolly. In the beginning the consistency of the mixture resembles mud. It is necessary to add iron chips into it gradually until the substance becomes like a thick medicine. The obtained substance should be put into a canvas bag and place the bag on a wooden bench or stool.

Each morning you must deliver various, even though spontaneous and irregular blows at a bag on the bench. The blows should be light and heavy, slow and quick, touching blows and blows directed inside. It is up to the trainee to decide which kind of blows to deliver. At the first stage of training swelling can appear on your hand, but later when the skin on damaged parts changes, the hand will become insensitive to blows. After training in delivering blows, it necessary to wash hands with special medicine which cures swelling and makes the muscles and the skeleton stronger, strengthens the body outside and inside.

After training during 100 days, you will be able to employ the skill TIE SHA ZHANG. After training during one year you will obtain great mastery. But do not abuse and do not use the skill you learnt for the evil, but for the good. That pugilistic art

---

Editor's notes:

[100] That is about two hours.

strengthens skin and muscles and allows to easily deliver heavy blows which can be fatal for the enemy. If you don't use the medicine, training will take much more time. It might be as well to use the medicine for averting body damages and strengthening oneself from inside.

Usually one starts learning that skill to use it for future defense of the state against an assault of enemies. If you learn that skill, it is necessary to be anxious about common weal and interests of the state, but not about personal interests. One should not start training alone, as only a fierce wolf kills its pray so as to be unnoticed.

When you exercise in TIE SHA ZHANG, you develop the YANG force in your body, but that method also allows to strengthen the YIN force contained in an arm. When you use the medicine, the "force" contained in it penetrates deep into arm muscles. So, if you use the medicine, you may not smear the hands with ointment MI FAN after you have finished to deliver blows. If the skin of the hand swells or begins to fester in several days, use the ointment in that case and stop training for some time. After the application of the ointment the skin on hand, muscles and bones must become stronger, such a hand can be called "poisonous hand" (DU SHOU). Sometimes the "poisonous hand" is called GANG SHA ZHANG which means "Palm of Steel Sand". That skill is also called TIE SHOW FEI SHA, "Iron Hand of Flying Sand" or HEI HU SHOU, "Hand of Black Tiger".

As time passed, all left from that skill were hieroglyphs in books. Secret techniques which were kept in secret during many centuries are available for a common use now. But those who have been not initiated have no right to teach or advise. When the conversion of the skill into word was finished, people have known only its name, but they have not seen it in action. Really, does not it cause a regret? It is necessary not only to listen words of tutors, but also deepen the true knowledge in the field of WU SHU, investigate and study that ancient Martial Art. However, one does not have to be in hurry.

The skill "Palm of Iron Sand" possesses a huge power which is comparable with the power of fire-arm. But if you try to unite both forces into one, you can cause harm to yourself, as you have to respect individual and unique way of each force. That law is also true for the society. After understanding it in time and being convinced in huge curing ability of the ointment, you will not use the skill "Palm of Iron Sand" maliciously. You must always realize that you are able to break off the thread of human life. Indeed, with the "Poisonous Hand" you can cut the enemy's head or cause serious body damages.

48. Pulling a Silk Thread (YI XIAN CHUAN)

This exercise has another name "Da Mo crosses the river"[101]. It is also called "Flight over water". The common name is "Walking on a cord". It is the skill (GONG FU) that is called "Going over a water obstacle on small duckweed" (DENG PING DU SHUI) and "Walking on snow without leaving traces" (TA XUE WU HEN) in novels about knights. The skill belongs to a section of exercises "Light body" (JIN SHEN SHU), it is "soft" and develops the internal power.

Editor's notes:

[101] Da Mo, Bodhidharma is an Indian preacher, the first patriarch and the founder of Zen Buddhism (Chan Buddhism in the Chinese transcription) in China. According to a legend he crossed the river of Yangtse on a straw and settled down at the monastery of Shaolin where he taught monks.

The method of acquiring the skill is far from being easy, but one can gain success if he exhibits a strong will. The training process consists of several stages. At the first stage it is necessary to train yourself in the same way as in the exercises "Skill of Flight" (FEI XING GONG)[102] and "Skill of Light Body" (JIN SHEN SHU)[103], that is to tie small bags with lead shot around legs and run at a flat ground at first and then train jumps on mountain roads. Later, put stones into a flat and wide wicker basket and go on its edges. It is necessary to remove stones from the basket gradually. If you are able of going on the edges of the empty basket without stones, you can proceed to training on a sand track. Those methods have been already discussed in detail in other exercises, namely in the exercises "Skill of Flight" and "Skill of Light Body". Moreover, as mentioned earlier, lead shot before being tied around legs must be treated in pig's blood to make lead "dead"[104]. The initial weight of small bags with lead shot which are tied around ankles is 200 g, the weight must be gradually increased to 2.5 kg. The ankles after training should be washed in a special solution GOU QI (equal parts of Lycium Chinese and salt are boiled) to avoid their damage. Then you train yourself by going on window paper: lay window paper on a sand track, 3 or 4 CUNs (10-13 cm) wide. You must train yourself until no traces are left. In that case the first stage will be over.

Editor's notes:

[102] See par. #53.
[103] See par. #44.
[104] See detail concerning that in par. #43.

After it take a thin and long stick and fix it at a height of 2 or 3 CHIs (0.70-1.0 m) from the ground. Train yourself in fast going on that stick. At first the stick strongly sags, but achieve that the stick will not to sag and will not spring, but remain absolutely immobile. Then, replace the stick with a thick rope. It is necessary to put two stands at some distance from each other and to tie the ends of the rope to them. Train yourself in walking on the rope as some do in a circus. As the rope is soft, it sags and swings when you step on it, therefore it is more difficult to go on it than on a wooden stick. Train yourself until the rope stops swinging. The second stage in acquiring the skill is over.

Starting from that moment, it is necessary to decrease the diameter of the rope gradually. When you are capable of walking freely on a cord with the thickness less than a finger so that it will not swing, it means the third stage is over. After that, replace the cord with the thinnest one and obtain the same result. After that it is necessary to stretch a rope across a river. If you can freely go on it even in this case, you have gained full success. Now you can go on the surface of a pond, though you need to use some thing, for instance a bamboo splinter, wooden small stick, reed etc. Place it on water surface, stand on it and advance! If duckweed, water grass, water chestnut or lotus grow in a pond, you can walk on them too. Once upon a time our forerunner Da Mo crossed a river alone on one reed after the sermon of his teaching. That is really the present type of GONG FU. It takes more than 10 years of labor to attain the aim. It is necessary to train yourself quietly and diligently.

49. Method of drawing in
YIN (XI YIN GONG)

The method of drawing in YIN is the "soft" GONG FU, it deals with the "internal" training and belongs to the YIN category. The purport of the method is to learn to draw in the left and right testicles into the lower part of the abdomen with a direct flow of QI to avoid their damage by the enemy. During the first stage of training it is necessary to be quiet and serene, eliminate all extraneous thoughts and move QI through the whole torso up to the lower part of the abdomen. Then, raise QI up. Move QI up and down in cycles in such a way. It can be repeated several times a day, but do not overstrain yourself extremely, otherwise you can harm your health and QI may be in decline. During the first sessions of training you will not have any unusual feelings. But over some time, when you descend QI into DANTIEN, the scrotum will become inflated like a ball. When you direct QI up, the testicles follow it and finally come to the lower part of the abdomen. Outside is only the scrotum. Therefore, enemies will not be able to damage them. In that case you have gained the complete success. Thus, when raising QI up, the testicles are drawn into the abdomen, and when descending QI, the scrotum becomes hard, which also protects the testicles.

50. Technique of Rubbing and Thrusts (MO CHA SHU)

The technique of "Rubbing and Thrusts" belongs to "hard" and "external" exercises, it is "hard" Yang force as to its character, but at the same time it also strengthens the inner spirit. The training method is rather simple and understandable, that skill is used in such techniques as "Methods of impact on acupoints" (DIAN XUE SHU), "Methods of impact on bones" (YU GU FA) and other basic methods of Gong Fu.

The method of training is as follows. Stand up and put feet together at the first gleam of light in the East. It is necessary to stand freely, close the mouth and "hide the tongue"[105], reach complete composure. After jointing both palms, rub them 20 times on each other. At first, lay the right palm on the center of your chest, and the left palm on

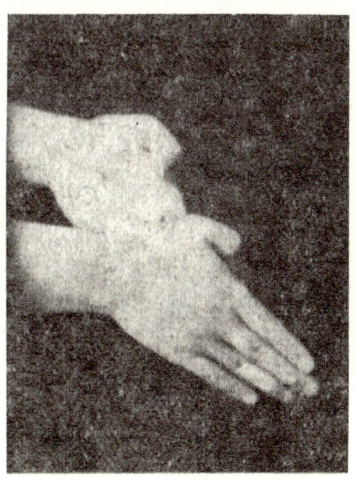

Editor's notes:

[105]"Hide the tongue" means that the mouth is closed, the tongue is behind teeth and touches the upper palate.

your spine. Thus, both palms face each other. Do 40-50 rubbings with palms, making circular movements. Then, move the right palm to the back and the left palm to the center of the chest and do 40-50 rubbings as above described. You must not breathe out through the mouth, use the nose for breathing, imagine how the breast is filled with QI.

After some quite long time you will feel the single refined QI roll into a ball, QI concentrates in the chest like a pulsating pearl ball. Wait until the ball increases and fill the whole chest. In that case the refined QI reaches the surface of the breast and begins to inspissate. From here QI moves very slowly to both hands and from the hands reaches finger tips.

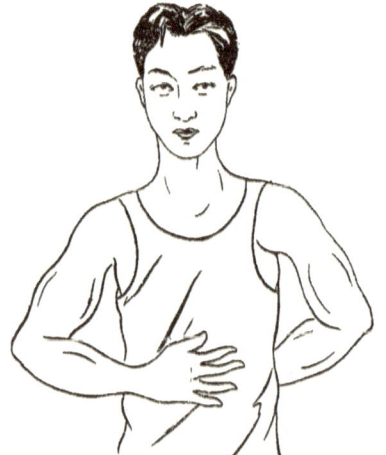

Then, take a box filled with beans and make thrusts with fingers. Both hands move in turn, one hand raises, the second one lowers, number of repeated movements in the exercise depends upon physical ability of a trainee. It is necessary to do the exercise until painful feeling appears. One should keep in mind the number of thrusts and gradually, day after day, increase them. For example, do 100 times during the first day, 105 times

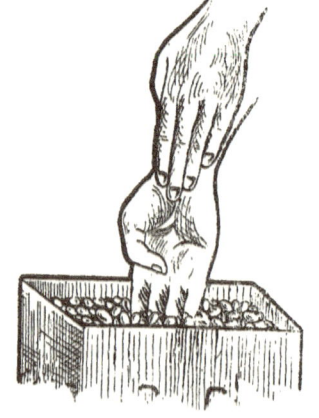

during the second day and increase the duration of this exercise gradually to the time needed for burning off an aromatic stick[106]. That is the first stage in obtaining mastery. After that, beans should be replaced with rice grains, continue to do the exercise as before and increase the duration of the exercise to the time needed for burning off an aromatic stick. That is the end of the second stage. Now a box with rice should be replaced with a box with sand, continue to train yourself according to the same pattern and use the time of burning off an aromatic stick as a guidance. At that stage you will reach full success in mastering the skill MO CHA SHU.

As mentioned before, the exercise should be done before getting into bed and at dawn. After its acquirement it is necessary to learn the technique of point impact DIAN XUE SHU, and after it you will be able to use your mastery in practice more effectively. After practising the exercise during one year it will be possible to learn the technique of point impact, and it will be the second level of mastery. Training and strengthening fingers is a base, it is impossible to reach full success in learning the point technique DIAN XUE SHU without it.

A wooden box for that exercise should be made of unabi tree or elm, its area should be two square CHIs (about 50 x 50 cm), its height may be about one CHI (33 cm). The box is

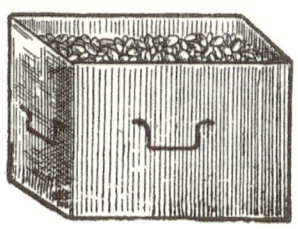

Editor's notes:

[106] Apparently about 40 minutes, although the original text does not give any indications as to the size of an aromatic stick.

filled with soybeans, then common rice, then yellow sand (or yellow clay). When you acquire steady skills, you can proceed to iron filings and gradually increase the duration of training session to the time needed for burning off an aromatic stick. After that your fingers will become as hard as iron and you will be able to make a hole in a chest or tear stomach muscles. It is strictly obligatory to wash your hands with heated medical solution after finishing the exercise with iron filings to eliminate swelling and damages in such a way, it is necessary to pay a great deal of attention to it.

51. Exercise "Stone Pile" (SHI ZHU GONG)

It is necessary to start from a main basic exercise. There is such an exercise of utmost importance in each school and each style of Martial Arts. Pile!

The exercise "Stone pile" is a "hard" exercise which strengthens the "internal". It belongs to basic methods of the "pile"-style exercises that specialize in strengthening legs and is one of orthodox exercises. That exercise has such a name because legs of those who train it become like steadfast piles when the trainees reach the highest degree of its acquirement. Even people who have great physical strength can not throw (you) off your balance.

The man who practises a Martial Art pays a great attention to leg strength because if legs are weak, movements will be unsteady, and if movements are unsteady, there will be no way to victory. At the first stage, when leg strength is trained, one must train oneself in the stance of "Rider". It is necessary to take stance of "Rider" at least ten times every day and be in it at the initial stage not long. It is necessary to increase gradually the time in the stance and decrease

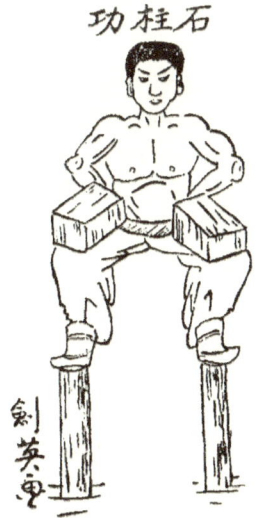

repetitions of the exercise respectively. When you bring the time of remaining continuously in the stance to one hour and feel no tiredness, it means that the initial target has been reached and you can proceed to the next stage.

Later, it is necessary to exercise in standing on piles. Dig two piles into the ground, their height should be about two CHIs (about 66 cm) and the distance between them should be equal to the width of the "Rider" stance. Stand on the piles and train yourself as before, taking the stance of "Rider". When you stood on the ground, the whole sole of the foot touched the ground and the force was equally distributed, as the surface of the ground is big. Now, when you stand on the poles, the surface to which the force is applied decreased and limited by the top of the piles. Therefore, the surface of force application is much less than when you stand on the ground, less than one third of a foot sole. The full degree of difficulty can not be expressed with words. At the initial stage, when you stand on the piles, it is difficult to use the strength of both legs, the whole body is unsteady and the central part of the sole hurts, you are not able of standing even during one minute. You must firmly endure difficulties, persistently train yourself and after three months painful feeling will gradually disappear and in that case the time for doing the exercise can be gradually increased.

Some time later you will feel that your whole body will be filled with QI that utters a drumming sound like a beat of drum. That QI should be lowered depending on the direction of efforts of your whole body as if you wish to "split" the foothold. In that case the stance will improve so that it will be possible to lay a stone slab weighing 1000 JINs (about 500 kg) on your hips. To obtain such a result, take rectangular stones and lay one piece on the right hip and another piece on the left one, you may hold them with your hands. In the beginning the weight of the used stones must be 20 – 30 JINs (10 – 15 kg). It is necessary to add by 10 JINs (5 kg) during each three months and gain ability to bear a weight of 100 JINs (50 kg) and more. When you are able to stand on the piles in the stance of "Rider" during half an hour without being tired and without sweating, it means that training yielded some success but the strength of both legs is insufficient to hold a weight of 1000 JINs (500 kg) and you have to continue training.

After that, if you stand on a flat surface, you look like bronze or cast iron which took roots. And if several men try to throw you off balance, they will be like a dragon-fly trying to shake loose a stone pole. Seldom you will come upon a man who will be capable of moving you a little bit. Both legs attain incomparable firmness, their strength so differ from the legs strength of ordinary people that it frightens them. But burden and deprivations while training that exercise are awful, they are greater than in other kinds of Gong Fu. It takes a lot of time to do the exercise and it needs long training, 5 or 6 years at least. The learner who is not fearless and without strength of mind, whom hardships frighten, will not be capable acquire it completely. Many who start to train that exercise, after some short time, about half a month, feel very sharp pain in their legs and stop half way. My Tutor deeply regrets about it.

52. Skill "Neither Lances nor Broadswords Can Wound" (QIANG DAO BU RU FA)

Skill "Neither Lances nor Broadswords Can Wound" is a "soft" GONG FU, has the "outer" power, belongs to the force YIN and at the same time YANG as to its essence and spirit confined in it. That method seems to be somewhat enigmatic and mysterious. But in reality, it is simply one of training methods in a "soft" GONG FU.

Sometimes, for instance, such words can be heard: "I can engage with empty hands a mob armed with the sword DAO and halberd JI and they can not even wound me". Usually listeners of those words think it to be absolutely absurd. However, people who acquired that kind of GONG FU to perfection really can do so.

Training in that skill is quite difficult. More over, few people have that skill now, that method is practically lost. The purport of the method is in dodging and avoiding. It is necessary to start from training the skill "Soft Bones" (see par.#32) which includes such exercises as "flexible legs", "flexible waist" and so on. Besides, it is necessary to train your eyes for distance estimation. Training body, arms, and eyes is the most important principle in WU SHU. It is possible to enter a "forest" of swords and lances and leave it without being wounded only thanks to an eye skill. Otherwise, it is difficult to confront such a situation. First steps in training eye sight have been already described in the exercise "Luohan's skill" (see par.#23). Later, it is necessary to train oneself in counting immovable objects. For example, you sit in a room, look in the window and count bricks in the wall of the opposite house. Or, you can count number of tiles on the roof in each row. Try to cast a quick glance and say the exact number, it is not so simple. You can make piles of tiles or other objects with a height of several CHIs[107] and count them. If you can exactly count in a short time, you can go further.

Now it is necessary to count moving objects, for instance, ducks swimming in a river. They may be a hundred, a little bit more or less. Tiles are immovable things, they lay at one place: count them attentively and you do not make a mistake. But ducks in a river are swimming here and there all the time, so it is not a simple task to count them at once. One can gain success here

---

Editor's notes:

[107] 1 CHI is equal to 0.33 m.

only by hard labor and concentration of attention. As they say, mastery comes with experience and achieved by labor. It takes about half a year. Later, it is necessary to proceed to count objects of smaller size, for instance, sparrows. Replace gradually objects to be counted with smaller ones. You may proceed from sparrows to dragon-flies. After dragon-flies, count grasshoppers, beetles, ants at last. If at a distance of five steps you can count a heap of ants numbered two or three thousand, it means you reached the highest keenness of sight.

Besides the eye-sight, it is necessary to exercise legs and body. Training on poles[108] suits well for that. There are many exercises of this kind: "Poles of Three Treasures" (SAN CAI ZHUANG), "Poles of Seven Stars" (QI XING ZHUANG), "Poles of Nine Stars" (JIU XING ZHUANG), "Poles of Plum Blossom" (MEI HUA ZHUANG) and others. All those methods are suitable. After training on poles one may proceed to direct acquirement of "Skill of Dodging Lances and Broadswords". First of all, it is necessary to choose a ground and install bamboo and wooden sticks of different thickness and height. They should be placed at random. Lime should be also spread on the ground at random. The distance between neighboring sticks should not exceed 1 CHI.

The purport of training is that it is necessary to go fast between the sticks without touching them and without stepping lime. It should not be a walk on a preset route but a chaotic walk, at

---

Editor's notes:

[108] See in detail about it in par.#28.

random. Figuratively speaking, "like a butterfly flying among flowers, like a snake slithering in the grass". At first it is not, of course, easy and the speed is not great. But over time the speed of movements will increase and you will be able to go easily and freely and turn to any side. After that, it is necessary to fix knives and other sharp things on the sticks and lay iron prickles on the ground. If you can freely "enter" and "leave" even now, it means the full success. Now, even if a few dozens of armed people attack you alone, all the same you will not be wounded. However, it takes not less than 10 years of hard work to improve your mastery to such a level. It is useful to have that skill, as you will not be afraid of meeting bad people. In case you can easily to take away weapon from your enemy. That kind of GONG FU was passed over only at the Shaolin Temple. At the present time very few people learn it and that skill is almost lost. That causes a deep regret.

53. Gong Fu "Flight" (FEI XING GONG)

The other names of GONG FU "Flight" are "Skill of Night Walking", "Method of Flight over the Earth", and "Solitary Walk of 1,000 LIs". It is a "soft" GONG FU which develops the "internal" power, it belongs to the section of exercises called "Light body" (JIN SHEN GONG).

The training method is as follows: fill fabric bags with lead or iron shot and tie them to legs. Run quickly on a flat ground until you exhaust. In the beginning the weight of shot (it should be treated with pork blood)[109] must not be great. Later, add periodically, in every few days, one LIANG (50 g) until the weight of shot on each leg reaches 4 or 5 JINs (2 – 2.5 kg). It is difficult a little at first, but if you go with this load 50 km each day, in several years later nobody can run down you if you walk without bags with shots. But to go on a flat ground by day is not yet enough. If you can go at night on a rugged ground or on a ground with sheer rocks and cliffs as fast and adroitly as on a flat ground, you can be sure that the full success has been achieved.

Editor's notes:

[109] See detail concerning that in par.#43, "Skill of Tortoise Back" (GUI BEI GONG).

After taking off bags with shot you will feel the lightness of your body, you can jump over high walls, climb almost impassable mountains. The method for training night sight is described in detail in the exercise "LUOHAN"[110]. It is better to exercise that kind of Gong Fu without haste, no need to be in hurry, it is necessary to train oneself in consecutive order, constantly, steadfastly, and continuously. Otherwise you will not only succeed, but will receive body damages. After gaining the full success and if you acquired the method of high and long jumps you will be able to go as fast as if flying on ridges of roofs and tops of walls. You have reached the top in mastery.

Editor's notes:

[110] See par.#23, "LUOHAN GONG".

54. Hand of Five Poisons (WU DU SHOU)

Another names of the skill WU DU SHOU is "YIN Hand" and "Palm of Five Thunders". It is a "hard" GONG FU, it develops the "external" power and belongs the YANG category, but at the same time also contains "softness" YIN. Many wanderers exercise that kind of GONG FU.

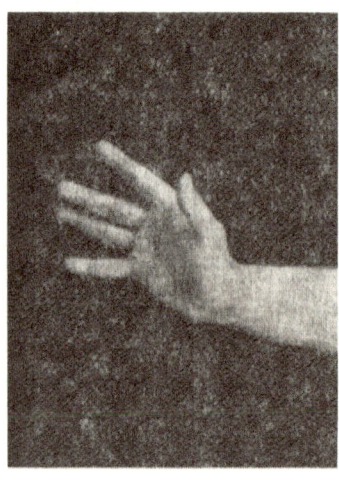

The method is very simple, you need only to get ready for training. On the eve of Qing Ming festival[111], dig out a lower layer of clay weighing 10 kg. The clay should be of light yellow color. Put it into an earthenware vat for drying. During the festival Duan Wu[112] put a red snake, a gecko, a spider, a toad, and scolopendra into clay, that is so called "five poisons". Pound them together with clay. Add then 5 kilogram of iron shot into clay, 5 kg of vinegar, 2.5 kg of strong spirit, 1 kg of bronze shot. Place the obtained mass on a bench. Strike at it

---

Editor's notes:

[111] 4 - 6 April.
[112] 5-th of May according to the lunar calendar.

every day in the morning and in the evening. If you train yourself in consecutive order and tirelessly, you will get success in three years. If a man is struck by such an arm, he can perish, therefore such a blow can not be thoughtlessly delivered. To avoid delivering such a blow unintentionally, it is better to exercise the left arm. The hands after training must be washed with special solution prepared according to a secret recipe. Otherwise in three days the hand begins to rot and no cure will help.

55. Skill of Water Separation (FEN SHUI GONG)

FEN SHUI GONG is a "hard" GONG FU, has external power, belongs to the YANG category. There are the following sections in WU SHU: "Methods of Sweeping off Obstacles" (PAI SHAN SHI) and "Palm Separating Water" (FEN SHUI ZHANG). Skill of Water Separation is the very origin of those GONG FU. The strength of that GONG FU is concentrated in both arms, palms are of auxiliary significance.

At the first training stage, it is necessary to take bamboo, a little more than ten sticks and fix them at the upper and lower part with an iron chain. Do not leave clearance between the sticks, put them closely one to another like a wall. The trainee puts his palms together and introduce them between the middle sticks of bamboo. Bamboo is flexible and resilient. Although there is no space between the sticks, but if you apply force, you can move them apart. After the introduction of palms, it is necessary to move arms aside with strength. In the beginning there appears a small clearance but over time the clearance will increase to the size of a door so

that a man can easily pass through it. After that, it is necessary to increase the number of sticks to several dozens and make efforts to pass easily through the bamboo wall. It means you are on the way to the full success.

When you add one more bamboo stick, the effort to be applied should be 50 kg more. Let's suppose that you put 30 bamboo sticks, in that case the force of arm pressure should exceed 500 kg. Then, build a sand wall or use a clay wall in your village. Put your hands into the wall and spread them to sides. If even now you can easily spread your hands and bring them together, it means you have attained perfection and the training is a full success. The effect of combination of hard and soft GONF FU occurs. Even attacked by a large group of people, you raise your hand – it looks like a mountain moving or a tsunami rising. Each whom your hand touches will fall down.

56. To Fly Up to the Ridge and to Walk on a Wall (FEI YAN ZOU)

The skill of "To Fly Up to the Ridge and to Walk on a Wall" is also called "Eight Steps in the Horizontal Position" (HENG PAI BA BU). It is a soft Gong Fu, it develops the internal power and belongs to one of kinds of "Light Body" exercises. The secret technique of that method was passed over only by monks of the Shaolin monastery.

The training method is very simple. Tie small bags of coarse fabric with iron shot (treated in pig blood) to your arms and legs. The weight of those bags are small in the beginning. You

have to run on a wall in the horizontal position every day. Touch down when you are exhausted. It is done in such a way: stand at a distance over 10 steps from a wall, take a running start and, using inertia, step on the wall so that the body takes the horizontal position. It is necessary first to make a step with your left foot and then at once with the right one. Any young man can make two or three steps in such a position, sometimes even three or four steps, but not more. When inertia of your body runs low, touch the ground with your right foot immediately. At the same time the body passes from the horizontal position to the vertical one. It is the left-side variant of that method. There is also the right-side variant when the right foot first steps on a wall and the left foot first touches the ground when landing. It is necessary to exercise every day and to increase gradually the weight of shot in the small bags.

One year later, moving along the horizontal line, that is parallel to the ground, you will be able to make four or five steps. It means that a preliminary success has been made. One more year later you will be able to make eight steps. It is the second stage on the way to success. The length of eight steps is equal to 1.6 ZHANG approximately (about 5.3 m). It means that you will be able to go 1,6 ZHANG in the horizontal position (and along the horizontal line) due to the force of impulse. Then, proceed to exercise walking on a wall along an inclined line. At first you will fall, but it is necessary to train oneself day after day and overcome all obstacles. Increase at the same time the weight of iron shot up to 6 kilograms. One year later you will be able to make 8 steps along an inclined line. It will mean that the third stage is over. It is necessary, then, to train yourself in waving arms: left-right and right-left. It is done in such a way: you run to the top of a wall along an inclined line, but at that moment your body is still in the horizontal position, inertia already ran low, so it is necessary to wave the left arm to the left and downward strongly and abruptly, the right arm also moves to the left side. The effort emerging at that time makes the body pass to the vertical position on the top of the wall. It concerns the left-side variant; if you first move the right arm, then the left one, it will be the right-side variant (see above). It will be the full success. You take off the small bags with iron shot and can move as easily and deftly as a monkey. It will be a trifle to climb walls and houses after that.

However, at the beginning of training you are not very deftly, therefore you often fall, but don't make a doubtful conclusion out of it. It is necessary to advance. The time for full success will come. In my childhood I trained myself, but then I spent a lot of time travelling and stopped training. I am very sorry about it. In a word, to acquire that kind of Gong Fu, it is necessary to realize deeply its importance.

57. Skill of Somersaulting (FAN TENG SHU)

This kind of Gong Fu belongs to the section of exercises "Light Body". It is also called "Leather Strips" - PI TIAO GONG. The purport of that method is: you can climb up and climb down if you have something to catch on. It is necessary to train first somersaults and other acrobatic exercises on the ground. It is obligatory for all those who practise WU SHU. We shall not dwell on length on it. Then, you exercise in pulling yourself up on a horizontal bar. Clasp the metal bar with both hands, pull yourself up slowly so that the lower part of the stomach should be at the same level with the bar. Climb down slowly then to the ground. Exercise the "windmill" after it – that is rotation round the bar.

The next step: replace the metal bar with a soft and flexible one. The point is that you train the strength of both arms on a metal bar, that is its purpose. If a bar is not rigid one, you can not use the centrifugal force while rotating round it. As to a soft and flexible bar, it is nothing else but leather strips. It is necessary to install two poles of three ZHANGs (about 10 m) high, the distance between the poles must be equal to two ZHANGs (6.6 m). A cross bar with a few metal rings is fixed on the top. The distance between neighboring rings must be two CHIs (0.66 m). Long leather strips hanging down up to the ground like fringe are tied to the rings. The trainee stands on the ground between leather strips and holds a strip in each hand. He starts to climb up: if he holds with his right hand, his left hand catches up, if his left hand holds, the right hand catches up. Do so up to the

uppermost point. Do the same for climbing down. Exercise in moving horizontally after that. If your training tool is arranged in the direction from East to West, you have to grasp the first and second strips starting from the eastern side, climb up to the middle, release the first strip, face the West and grasp the third strip, release the second strip, grasp the fourth strip an so on. Move in the western direction in such a way and reach the last strip, then move back. Train yourself so until your strength exhausts. Some time later, you may start exercising rotation almost in the same way as on a metal bar, the difference is not big. It is easier to do that exercise fast than slowly. Therefore, it is recommended to gradually proceed from a fast execution of that movement to slow one. It is necessary to succeed in doing that exercise with ease.

The next training stage is movement with lowered arms. It is done as follows: each hand squeezes a strip, you apply downward effort and your body ascends. Simultaneously both hands release the strips and immediately catch up. Do so up to the uppermost point. Climb down in the same way. Exercise then in jumping over in the transverse direction (as regard to the strips). That method resembles the above-described method of horizontal movement. But now it is necessary not to move in succession of the leather strips, that is not to catch the neighboring strip, but skip a few strips. For instance, you are between the first and second strip from the eastern side, climb up to the middle, make a swing to the western side and catch the fifth and sixth strips and so on. After acquiring all those methods you may replace the leather strips with a finger-thick silk cord. Continue to exercise in such a way, but decrease periodically the thickness of the cord so that at last it should be not thicker than a chopstick. If even in that case you are able to

do the above exercises, one can say that you have reached perfection in the skill. You will be able to climb on any complicated surface where is something to catch. That kind of Gong Fu is quite difficult, at any rate, it demands 6 or 7 years of training. Many fireman exercise it. I saw my friends showing that kind of Gong Fu. It was a beautiful show.

58. Pole of Cypress (BAI SHU ZHUANG)

"Pole of Cypress" is a hard Gong Fu, it develops the external power and belongs to the YANG category. That method is intended for the development of kicking force, mainly fighters exercise it. It is also a base exercise for specialists in WU SHU in five northern provinces. The training method is very simple and its purport is as follows: dig a pole into the earth with more than a half of its length outside. Make kicks and pushes with both legs in succession, imagining that the enemy is in front of you and it is necessary to hit at his vital points. At first your legs will hurt, but the pain will gradually disappear. Half a year later your legs will be more or less trained, and a year later the force of legs will exceed the force of legs of ordinary people by far. When kicking, QI supports the force. If you stand "holding" QI, three men will not be able to budge you. The enemy kicked with such a leg falls down. It means the first step has be made.

Replace then the pole with a special stone in the shape of a rectangular parallelepiped with a narrower top weighing 250-350 kilograms. At first your legs will hurt but the pain will disappear over time. Moreover, the stone will shift to a distance of several CHIs[113] as a result of a kick. It means the aim has been achieved. Everything depends upon diligence and persistence of trainees.

Editor's notes:

[113] 1 CHI = 33 cm.

59. Ba Wang's Elbow (BA WANG ZHOU)

There is no such an exercise which could be compared with this one. It is not more than a killing technique and it is difficult to save life even with a medicine. Therefore, each man who exercises this method must be extremely careful.

The exercise "Ba Wang's[114] elbow" belongs to "hard" exercises aimed at external strengthening of the body. It is of YANG "hard" kind. That method is one of exercises to strengthen and fortify the elbows. However, that exercise differs from the exercise "Eagle Wings" (see par.#37) where the side surface of an elbow is used, as well as some parts of forearms and shoulders close to an elbow. "Ba Wang's Elbow" is a special exercise where an elbow tip is strengthened to deliver downward and backward blows. Those two exercises must not be confused.

At the first stage of doing that exercise it is necessary to lie down on the ground completely, face up, bend arms in elbows so that forearms may be placed vertically and the front surfaces

---

Editor's notes:

[114] Ba Wang, a High Prince, one of titles in the ancient China, figuratively "despot", "evildoer".

of fists pointed up, set heels with strength against the ground, both legs being stretched. "Send" then force to both elbows and set them with strength against the ground rising the body above the ground. Thus, except elbows and feet all other parts of the body are "suspended" in the air for some time. Then, sink down and have a little rest. When the body is rising, it is necessary to regulate breath, you must not breathe irregularly. **If you have irregular breath, the energy QI can not concentrate and the physical force LI will be also dissipated**[115]. In that case you can not maintain that position for a long time. The exercise should be done every day, one time in the morning and in the evening, do it several dozens each time and increase number of executions gradually. During the day time it is necessary to knock with elbows on hard objects from time to time for strengthening elbows and better acquirement of the exercise.

At the second training stage, after the body having risen it is necessary to turn so that only one elbow and one foot may support your body. For example, place first the left hand on the waist and be supported by the right elbow and the right foot. To do that, turn the whole body to the right slowly and the body will take the position "lying on a side". Maintain that position until extremely painful feeling appear and return then to the initial position. Next, after directing force into the left elbow and the left foot, turn the torso to the left and take a left-

---

Editor's notes:

[115] A special prominence was given to that phrase by the author in the original text.

- 238 -

side position "lying on a side". Continue to do the exercise to each side several dozens of times in such a way and finish the exercise with that. But that is not enough. After training the exercise on a clay soil during one year when your body is stable in a side position, proceed to do the exercise on a stone slab. Use a rough stone slab for that purpose later. To continue training, dig a recess, 3 CHIs (about 1 meter) wide and 6 CHIs (about 2 meters) long, fill it with pebbles of different size and fix them with mortar of clay and sand poured into the recess so that the pebbles may form a single monolith. Continue to exercise on protruding pebbles as before. Sharp painful feeling is unavoidable in the beginning, but it is necessary to train yourself in the same way as on a flat ground and at last you will feel no painful feeling and tiredness at all. It is necessary to continue lessens persistently to reach such a state. Use medical tincture to wash elbows and cure bone damages.

Proceed to use stones with prominent ribs later and also fix them with clay and sand. Train yourself in the same way to be insensitive to pain when you do the exercise. Over time both elbows and both feet will become strong enough and will be like cast iron at last. They will become as sharp as a knife edge, a blow will become as strong as a blow of a big hammer and you yourself will receive no harm. In that case, if you strike at the enemy, you will break through his chest or squash his stomach. You have to spend 3 years from the beginning to the end of the exercise.

60. Exercise "Pinching a Flower" (NIAN HUA GONG)

It is a very refined exercise, but (it is necessary to keep) constancy! After successful acquirement (of the exercise) you can not only kill people, but effect on acupoints with your fingers like needles used in ZHEN JIU[116] and save human life.

The exercise "Pinching a flower" belongs to "soft" exercises for "external" strengthening. It is the YIN "soft" force as to its kind. It is one of exercises which specialize in strengthening finger tips, small parts in human extremities. Their strength is not comparable with that one of a fist or a palm, that's why they need training. It takes a lot of time and it is difficult to get success. But if your have strong spirit and train yourself for a long time without intervals, one of the days will bring you success. If after successful acquirement of the exercise you strike the enemy with your fingers, you can inflict a severe wound to him and if you strike with force, you can kill him.

Editor's notes:

[116] ZHEN JIU, Acupuncture, traditional method of the Chinese medicine which uses needles and cautery for curing diseases.

That exercise has direct resemblance to such exercises from the section "Deadly Hand" as "Saddle" (MA AN GONG, par.#62) and "Palm of GUANYIN"[117] (GUANYIN ZHANG, par.#70).

At the first training stage of the exercise "Pinching a flower" you need not to use any supporting means, you need only to closely put the forefinger and the middle finger together and press on them with your thumb. All three fingers come into contact together with their tips in the first phalange. Make screwing (rubbing) movements very slowly in the outside direction on a circle (anticlockwise). Then,  make certain number of screwing (rubbing) movements in the inside directions (clockwise), make after it certain number of screwing movements from inside to outside and so on. Number of movements to each side must be the same. For example, if rotation in the inside direction was done 100 times, rotation in the outside direction should be also done 100 times. Do it every day and do not limit number of repetition, do the exercise if you have spare time. If your fingers hurt, have a rest and then continue to do the exercise. For the present, do not use any tools, do not learn a lot of techniques at the same time. You

---

Editor's notes:

[117] GUANYIN, the Goddess of Mercy in Buddhism (AVALOKITESVARA).

can conduct lessens at any convenient place and time. It is not easy for a stranger to understand what you are doing, therefore the exercise is very convenient.

If you persistently train yourself during one year, the force in fingers will increase by several dozens of times. In that case you may start to use three soybeans of the biggest size, squeeze them with the thumb, the middle finger, and the forefinger as before and make rotating movements. It is practically impossible to use three beans at the same time in the beginning by turning (rolling) them between fingers, as they will fall off all the time. One can learn to do it through diligent training during one month. Continue to train yourself in the same way during one year. During that period of time, it is necessary to gradually increase time of training in pinching soybeans. Do one or two times every day in the beginning, gradually improve mastery, replace, if necessary, beans with new ones. It is necessary to reach such a condition when fingers squeeze three beans together, but do not use force at that and only rotate (roll) them with fingers. When the beans are reduced into powder, the first stage in acquirement of that kind of Gong Fu is over.

It is necessary to replace soybeans with pebbles[118] and continue training according to the same method. Try to reach by training that small pebbles may be reduced into powder by squeezing them in a pinch. Replace them later by more solid minerals[119]. It

---

Editor's notes:

[118] HUANG SHI in the original text, lit. "yellow stones", probably stones of some soft rocks.
[119] QING SHI, "green stone" in the original text, probably granite.

is of no importance how solid the stones are, they can be reduced into powder with fingers. That is the end of process of acquiring this kind of Gong Fu. You have to spend not less than 5 or 6 years from the beginning till full acquirement of the exercise. Training with an "empty hand" takes one year, pinching beans one more year, squeezing the "yellow stones" from half a year to two years. Training with "green stones" will take two or more years. Even if you make a progress in doing the exercise as fast as possible, it will take 5 years at least.

After successful acquirement of that Gong Fu it is of no importance how hard is a thing: you take it with fingers and break at once, nothing to say about blood vessels and muscles of (my or another man's) body. People often use fingers in everyday life and make various movements with them. When you reach perfection in that exercise, you can, accidentally and unwillingly, cause a body damage to a man or to some thing. Therefore, if a man exercises that kind of Gong Fu, it is necessary to use the left arm, do not use the right one. Other people and I use the left arm and comparatively few people use the right arm trying to do the least harm. One must be very careful in training and life. Those who are far from moral perfection and have not reached the sharpness of mind must not set their arms going and wounds people. It is strictly prohibited by any pugilistic school. It is possible to wound a man thoughtlessly, therefore, one needs to be extremely careful. For that reason respectful masters of Martial Arts taught people the techniques of "Deadly Hand" with reluctance, and they themselves trained only their left hand. The trainee who deeply learnt that technique must consolidate his will-power and always be exceptionally careful.

61. Exercise "Pushing a Mountain with Palm" (TUI SHAN ZHANG)

It is difficult to parry a weapon, but it is more difficult to create it. Persistence is needed.

The method "Pushing a Mountain with Palm" belongs to "hard" exercises for external strengthening, as to its kind it the YANG and "hard" force. It is a special exercise for the central part of a palm that trains the "ejection" of the force FA JIN[120] and at the same time trains "sudden ejection" of the force CU JIN[121]. Its efficiency lies in combination of methods of "hardness" and "softness". If after successful acquisition of the exercise even a man of great physical strength like a bull attacks you, you can leave an imprint on his body with your palm, easily knock him down so that he may be tossed to several ZHANGs[122] away only by pushing him with a hand. It is also possible to overwhelm the enemy by "loaning"[123] his strength, direct an enemy's attack to the void to prevent body damages.

Editor's notes:

[120] FA JIN, one of specific terms in WU SHU implying fast muscle contraction when a method is executed.
[121] CU JIN, an abrupt movement from a static position.
[122] 1 ZHANG = 3.3 m.
[123] "Loaning" or "borrowing" force, one of special terms in WU SHU. It implies that during an enemy's attack his force is turned against himself.

Whatever happens, you must not wound a man using the technique of the "Deadly Hand".

The training method of the exercise is as follows: make a support of hard wood in the shape of a long table with four legs, dig them deep into the earth so that they stand securely and are not shaky. The upper part of the support must be firm too. Two horizontal wooden beams jutting out a little over the surface of the desk top must be covered with iron sheets (tinplate). At the first stage, take a square piece of "green stone" weighing about 80 JINs (about 40 kg) and put it on edge of the table. Stand opposite the stone, make a step toward it and assume the stance "Bow and Arrow" (GONG QIAN BU). Meanwhile the upper part of the torso will be at a distance of 1,5 CHI (about 50 cm) from the stone. Push the stone with both palms directly (horizontally) before yourself. The exercise can be also done with one hand, hands being changed in turn at that.

When you make a push, it is necessary to use force of three parts of a arm: arm proper, wrist and palm. At the same time the upper part of the torso tilts forward and the weight of your whole body presses on the stone. Do not be in hurry to acquire the exercise quickly, you should persistently try to push off the stone and perfect your mastery from day to day. If you fail to move off the stone, you should imagine it and push. If you exercise for a long time, one day you can see the exhibition of mastery, when after bending elbows and pressing on the stone you abruptly "eject" force and push, the stone certainly move

to a few CHIs[124] or even to a longer distance. In that case it is necessary to return the stone to its place, increase the weight by 20-30 JINs (10-15 kg) and continue training trying to move the stone to the same distance with a hand(s) push. Then, add one more stone weighing 30 JINs (15 kg) and train yourself as before. Gradually increase the weight of stones, you may stop when total weight of stones reaches 300 JINs (150 kg).

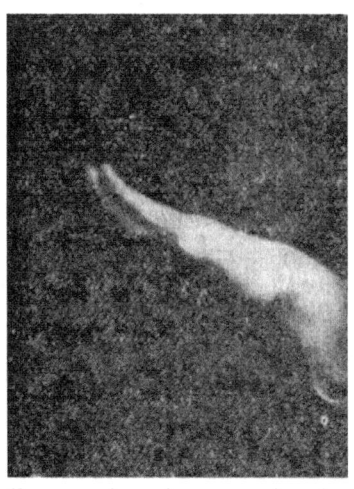

With that the first stage of acquiring the skill may be considered to be finished successfully. At that time you can see that force of both arms have reached the utmost limit, it becomes extremely hard in competition with another man's skill. You push him and get a stunning effect. It is necessary to selflessly create the foundation of the skill, if you make no progress in training "sudden effort" CU JIN, you can not fully acquire the exercise by making one more step. When training CU JIN, it is necessary to pay great attention to the lower part of the palm surface as well as to two parts – the hand and the wrist. The training method is, to a great extend, similar to the previous one: it is also necessary to move a stone lying on a support. Like in the initial

---

Editor's notes:

[124] 1 CHI = 33 cm.

exercise, one stone is used again, but the pushing technique somewhat differs. Now it is necessary to press on the stone surface with fingers and then push the stone from you with the lower parts of a palm. The position of the body is the same as described above. Force moves along the whole arm, from the forearm to the wrist. Before the execution of "ejection of force" fingers strongly press close to the surface of the stone, palms are in the horizontal position with the back side up. Thus, palms in the initial position are at a distance of not more than three CUNs (10 cm)[125] from the stone. You make a "sudden ejection of force" CU JIN from that position, push the stone with palms and move it. At the same time fingers raise up and remain in that position. Train yourself in that way every day. Each time when you strain yourself to the utmost, stop doing the exercise. After two years of hard training a stone weighing 80 JINs (40 kg) will be certainly thrown to a great distance. Continue training as before and add one more stone, go on adding stones up to the weight of 300 JINs (150 kg). At that stage GONG FU reaches its aim. If you engage an enemy, you will only slightly push him with the palm and he will be tossed away to a few meters.

That technique specializes in the use of the force JIN, therefore it does not damage a human body. After extending your mastery you can move a pile of several dozen stones lying on the support. You push one of the stones and the other stones are thrown away to several meters. Continue training and firmly

---

Editor's notes:

[125] That is actually at a distance of the finger length.

go toward the aim. Although, besides training FA JIN, "ejection of force", it is also necessary to extend mastery in XU JIN, "accumulation of force". Only the exercise "ejection of force" will take 4 years of hard training at least. If you exercise "accumulation of force", it will take 10 more years.

It is necessary to make a support for stone of hard wood, for example, chestnut-tree. The support should be 1.5 - 3 CHIs (0.5 – 1 m) wide, up to 3 ZHANGs (10 m) long, the height may be at the level of the waist. The shape of the support resembles a table, but it is a little bit lower. If you after successful acquirement of that exercise encounter a lot of enemies, you will be able to solve this problem simply. So-called "ejection of force" and "sudden effort" are refined methods that can not be described with a brush and Indian ink, sensation should be a guide in training, successive acquirement of the skill is needed.

62. Technique of Horse Saddle (MA AN GONG)

MA AN GONG serves for strengthening the outer power of the body and rearing the YANG force in it. Although the training method of the technique is relatively "soft", but you can not call the employment of that skill soft one, because when learning the skill MA AN GONG is over, your fist will become like an iron big hammer. A practitioner will be able to break stones with a hand as well as literally break through a human body, separate it into two halves. He will be able not only to make holes in different hard things but also inflict severe wounds on enemies who attacked him. However, it is always necessary to refrain from delivering deadly blows to the utmost and employ that skill only in cases of absolute necessity.

He who wants to acquire the skill must pay special attention and go into all possible peculiarities of fist employment in the exercise. When a fist is clenched, knuckles of fingers must be strictly on one line. The slightest deviation from that rule is not permissible. At the first training stage it is necessary to use a relatively light stone in the shape of a horse saddle. The weight of the stone should be about one JIN (0.5 kg). Every day it is necessary to make directed vertical blows with a straight arm and the same directed kicks at the stone. When the stone is knocked into the earth so deep that it can not be moved, it means that you have trained MA AN GONG for quite a long time. Then, you may proceed to exercise blows which make the stone "jump out" from the earth. You ought not to waste your strength for nothing. When you punch at the stone, it should move from a hand blow and shift from its place. Later you will be able to do the same with bigger stones.

If you master that training method with big stones, you will move stones weighing 100, 200 or 300 JINs (50, 100, and 150 kg respectively) from their place with ease. If you deliver blows each day during several years, you will make the heaviest stone "jump" from your blows.

When learning that technique comes to the successful end, it can be employed to inflict wounds of different severity and break or split various things. It is often enough to use only one hand in order to make damages and wound people. In ancient times WU SHU masters, when they taught people that skill, made special stress on training the left arm. But in our time people much oftener use rather the right arm than the left one, therefore one must try not to inflict pointless body damages and wounds on people.

63. Skill of Nephrite Belt (YU DAI GONG)

Even something that seems to be foolish or absurd can correspond to reality. If you make every effort and firmly endure difficulties for a long time, you will be able to attain the highest level of mastery.

The skill of Nephrite Belt serves for strengthening the external power of the body and rearing the YANG force in the body as well as for the development of the YIN "soft" force and the energy QI. The technique allows to "rotate", "collect", and "hold" various things using force of both arms; it is those methods that are to be learned to acquire YU DAI GONG. That technique has another name QIAN KUN JUAN - "The Continuous Round of the Universe".

The method of acquiring the exercise is quite simple. Choose in the beginning a tree around which you can easily put your arms. Stand just under it. Put your arms around it as tight as possible and clench fingers of both hands so that they can not come apart. Cling to the tree as close as possible and make such movements as if you try to raise it up. Meanwhile you must also press your knees to the tree from both sides, your posture is as if you squat and try to stand up with your arms around the heavy load. Do the exercise for a long time every day, make every effort while doing it. During one or two years your arms have to gradually gather strength and they will be finally filled

with it. You will become so strong that you will be able to tear off a tree from its roots, break its trunk and it will bleed sap. Then you will have a feeling that you have achieved a certain success in training, made a first step in acquiring the "Skill of Nephrite Belt". You will realize that you are on the way to defeat people.

When you are capable of uprooting trees, you will be able to proceed to exercises with big stones weighing up to 400-500 JINs (200-250 kg). It is more difficult to exercise with a stone: if you put your arms around it not close enough, it will slip in your hands. Train yourself until you can easily raise and lower the stone. When training in that part of the exercise is over, you may proceed to exercise the same movement with application of greater force. For that purpose you must not only raise and lower a stone but try to hold it suspended as long as possible.

After two years it is necessary to proceed to acquire the next part of the exercise. Its purport is to hold a stone in hands so that it may maintain the same position and to walk, squeezing it in both arms. In that case the body will be strengthened to the greatest extend and its strength will increase up to the highest mark. When you learn to hold a stone in arms and stand at one place for a long time squeezing a great weight in arms, you will easily hold a human body in your hands without inflicting significant damages on it. You will be able to hold a man without breaking his bones and without injuring his muscles.

There is one story about the "Skill of Nephrite Belt". Once upon a time lived a blind boy and he was eager to take vengeance on the enemies who had killed his father. As he was blind and lived alone, he could not learn the Martial Art and he cried bitterly because of it. Once the boy met a Shaolin monk who set out for a long journey. The monk heard his story and taught him the skill YU DAI GONG. After training during 4 or 5 years the boy acquired the technique so well that he could easily avenge himself on all enemies and forgot about his misfortune.

The technique of Nephrite Belt ought not be employed for a mere trifle. That skill is one of Shaolin secrets.

64. YIN Fist Method (YIN QUAN GONG)

Get to know the meaning of what you do before getting to know how all that is connected to the YANG force.

"The YIN Fist Method" that is also called the technique of "Well Fist" JING QUAN GONG is designed for the development of flexibility and body strengthening, it also permits to train the YIN force of the body.

During acquirement of that technique everything is aimed at training fists, therefore in ancient times the technique of "YIN Fist" was also called "YIN Hand" (YIN SHOU). When you practice the technique, it is necessary to come close to a well every day in the morning or after supper, stand in the stance of "Rider" (MA BU) in front of it and to punch applying force forward directly to the center of the well. Every day at least one hundred such blows must be made.

In the beginning you will feel no effect of practice sessions, but after one year or two years of continuous training barely audible splashes of water in the well will be heard each time when you punch above the well. Over time those sounds will become louder and more distinct. At that time you will be able to say that you have reached a high level of mastery. When the sound

of rough water is heard at a distance of a few CHIs[126] from the well, it will mean that you will be able to hit a man with your fist if he stands even at a distance of one or two ZHANGs[127] from you. The "soft" force YIN contained in the energy QI of a body can deeply penetrate into human bones and bring a man to death during several days.

In order to perfectly acquire that skill, you need at least 10 years, only after that time you will get a perceptible result. To acquire that technique, it is also possible to practice on a wall sending QI to it and moving away from it. That method has been used from the earliest times, but its employment can lead to some troubles[128].

It is possible to perfect in the YIN Fist skill using not only a well. Early in the morning before sunrise or late in the evening until the moon is risen, it is necessary to practice as follow: keep yourself on water surface without leaning anything and applying only the force YIN. In the past people called the Celestial Chambers as "Spring with well-water". Those Chambers were inhabited with various ghosts. If a blow was directed exactly to the center of a well, it could anger thousands of ghosts, therefore it was necessary to do extremely carefully in order not to harm fruit in the gardens of the Celestial Chambers. So all blows directed straightly to the center of a well were prohibited.

Editor's notes:

[126] One Chinese foot CHI is equal to 1/3 of a meter.
[127] One ZHANG is equal to 3.33 m.
[128] The meaning is not quite understandable, one may only suppose that a man can be affected by QI that reflects from the wall.

Blows could be delivered only in the direction of the well circle. Although it is only a superstition and it is not worth of so long discussion, some keep on following ancient behest to avoid any misfortunes. Meantime they defeat a man with an arm blow and think such a victory to be a virtue.

At first that skill seems to be outstanding, as great as the Sky and the Earth, but it is not marvellous at all. The Spirit fills the fist, the fist is filled with the YIN energy of QI, it permits to affect a man and inflict severe wounds on him. The skill was very effective in the past and by now it has not lost its importance.

65. Skill of Sand Bags (SHA BAO GONG)

Those who learn Martial Arts and always improve oneself in them make a lot for the development of all parts of the body, sight, and the technique of movement.

"Skill of Sand Bags" is aimed at strengthening the "external" power of the body and serves for rearing the YANG force in it. It also develops flexibility and mobility of the body. Thanks to this exercise the YANG force, adroitness and dexterity develop so much that it allows to defeat people easily.

Before starting to train yourself, dig into the ground four wooden poles and put four more wooden beams on the top. Fix bags with sand to each beam on the right, on the left, in front and in back. The weight of each bag should be about five or six JINs (about 2.5 – 3 kg). The bags must be tied to the beams with strong cord and hang loosely so that they can swing to sides freely. The bags must be at a height of man's shoulders.

The trainee stands in the center of the structure, assumes the stance of MA BU ("Rider") or GONG BU ("Bow and Arrow"). At first he delivers single punches at one of the sand bags so that the bag may fly out of the structure. When the bag returns back to the trainee, he has to strike at the bag again with greater force. One must be careful not to damage the wrist.

After mastering single blows it is necessary to proceed to punching with two fists. Strike at two bags simultaneously so that they may be thrown strictly forward. The right hand strikes at a bag, beats off the returning bag and so on. At that time the left hand acts in the same way. If a bag is moving from the right, it is more convenient to beat it off with the right hand rather than reach it with the left hand and vice versa. That exercise should be done 100 times at least during a day. Only that training rate ensures good acquirement of the movements. It is better to strike with both hands simultaneously and simultaneously receive bag blows with both hands. Then strike at bags again so that they may fly aside. Try to do those movements at the highest speed without pauses.

After acquiring the method of simultaneous blows at two bags one should start to strike successive blows forward, backward, to the right and to the left. When it is also acquired well, you may proceed to blows at four bags in any succession. One should especially attentive and see where blows are delivered. The body must be strictly between the bags. One should not ignore this recommendation.

After the acquirement of the four above-mentioned methods of striking at bags you may proceed to learn the two last methods. One of them is as follows: strike blows at bags which are on the right and the left, in front and in back and then, when the bags

return, beat them off using the force of your elbows. In the beginning the bags after blows will fly not too far, but when this part of the exercise is well acquired, the distance between the trainee and the bags will increase after each blow.

Below are described a few more methods of striking at sand bags. You can strike at bags with your head crown. At first, strike at bags which are in front and back of you and then at those ones that are on the left and on the right. Blows can be also delivered at sand bags with shoulders, those blows push apart the bags to the right and to the left. A trainee can strike at a bag behind him with back of his head. Thus, after acquiring all those methods one can simultaneously deliver blows at ten bags. At that stage "Skill of Sand Bags" can be regarded as mostly mastered.

Now it is necessary to exercise in the technique of delivering blows while walking, running, jumping, and being in the state of other motions. Such blows can be delivered not only with fists, but also with feet, shins, knees, shoulders, forearms, and other parts of the body. Each part of the body can and must be trained for making such blows. The blows must be struck to the right, to the left, forward, backward without stopping for a moment at one place, in that case the technique may be regarded as fully acquired.

If you find yourself encircled by a swarm of enemies and no man beside you who could shield you with his body, you can break out of the encirclement by striking practically with every part of your body as if you are encircled with a great lot of sand bags. In the past "Skill of Sand Bags" was one of simplest techniques that was learnt at the Shaolin monastery. It is one the most ancient techniques preserved till our days.

66. Skill "Piercing Through Stones" (DIEN SHI GONG)

It is possible to obtain a result only by making tremendous efforts and spending much time.

The skill "Piercing Through Stones" serves for strengthening the "external" power of the body, it is designed to rear the YANG force in a human body. That skill is aimed at training the "indicative force" of two fingers. After mastering it you can kill a man, just touching him with your hand. As regard to its effectiveness, it is similar to some "soft" exercises for finger training.

When you master the skill DIEN SHI GONG, you will be able to concentrate all your force in fingers, or in finger tips, to speak more correctly. Using only fingers, it is possible to do a lot of harm to the health of a man, moreover, it is possible to inflict severe wounds in him. You will be able to hit a man, even if some physical obstacle separates you from him. At that, it is necessary to indicate directly at the man

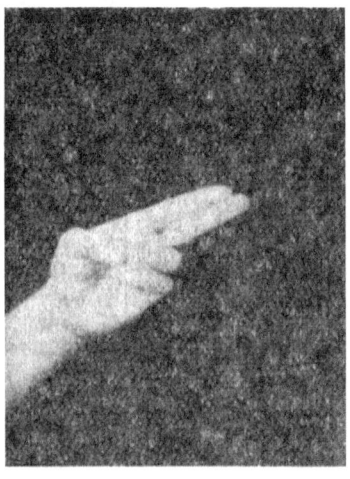

whose health you would like to do harm. Only in that case the use of that skill will have the highest efficiency. It should be realized well and kept in mind from the start of training. When you finish learning the exercise, you will be able to hit easily people only with your fingers and inflict on them severe wounds, even those ones that cause death. If one needs to cure such wounds with herbal medicine, he has to cure the whole body. If only fingers are capable of inflicting such body damages, what could you say about the whole arm and the destructive force which can be contained in it?

The method to acquire the skill is a simplest one. It is necessary to press two fingers (forefinger and middle finger) to each other and stretch them forward. The fourth finger and the little finger should be bent so that their pads may touch the center of the palm and be pressed strongly to it. The thumb should be pressed to the fourth finger and the little finger from above. Thus, the hand should look like that one squeezing the sword JIAN. Then, point finger tips that are stretched forward at some object and as if prick it with strength. That skill should be developed during many days.

It is best of all to train oneself in the beginning as follows: take some amount of soft soil, carefully pound it, mix it with liquid glue until it becomes stringy, wrap in a piece of cloth and leave it to dry up (to harden). Than draw a great number of small circles (on the cloth) with a middle-sized brush for writing hieroglyphs. Later, it will be necessary to thrust your fingers, fold as above, into the circles. At first, it is necessary to use one circle and prick it with fingers until a recess appears in it. Later, it will be necessary to make a recess in the second circle etc.

It is necessary to increase gradually number of exercises with each recess to make them ever deeper. So, daily number of exercises with each hole must reach ten. After two years of such training when you can easily pierce through the earth you may proceed to exercises with light stones. The principle of doing the exercises will remain the same as that one with earth.

Two more years later, when you can easily pierce through stones, the skill DIEN SHI GONG will have been mastered. At present this skill in use is as effective as in the past. Having acquired the technique, you yourself will have to understand the importance of this exercise for the Martial Art. Don't be blind, try to understand clearly the meaning of learning DIEN SHI GONG. The man who learns and improves the method must be very persistent from the very beginning. Training one of the skills of "Deadly Hand", he must concentrate his utmost attention to it without stopping to learn in no time. It is not so easy just to stretch an arm and inflict on a man such injuries that will cause death. Trainees who pay attention to all those things will master the skill "Piercing Through Stones" to perfection.

After it one may proceed to learn the skill of striking at vulnerable points DIAN XUE SHU to become more powerful.

67. Skill "Pulling Out a Mountain" (BO SHAN GONG)

It is necessary to free yourself from the "hard force" and there will be no ground for fear and anxiety.

The exercise "Pulling out a Mountain" belongs to the "hard" methods which strengthen the "internal" and at the same time develop the "soft" YIN force. The exercise is aimed at training the ability of "pulling out and holding" with the use of "empty force" (XU LI) of wrist. With this method, you will be able to win.

At the beginning, it is necessary to take a wooden pole, one ZHANG (3.3 m) long, make one of its ends pointed and dig securely into the ground to a half of its length approximately. Pour around it clay (or any mixture which can harden) with sand and small stones. The pole must stand very securely and should not become even a bit loose. Having done that preparation, it is necessary to hold strongly the 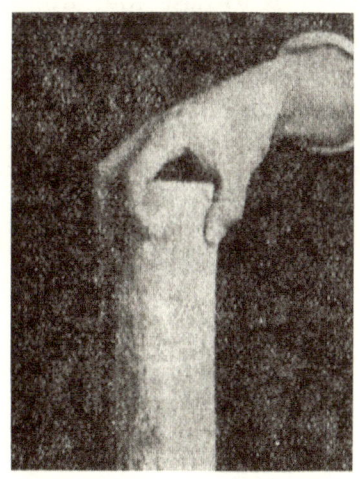 pole with three fingers (thumb, middle finger and forefinger)

every day and try to pull it up, applying all the strength. In the beginning the pole stands as strong as a mountain and in spite of all efforts no effect is seen. But keep constancy persistently, then fingers and the wrist will be stronger with every day. The pole gradually begins to move and rise up, when it is completely pulled out from the ground, the first stage of training is over. In the process of doing the exercise it is necessary to summon your strength and pull the pole up, the pole should not be shaken from side to side. The wooden pole being pulled up, use an iron pole, dig half of it into the ground and exercise. At training time to pull the iron pole from the ground. At that stage the "hard" Yang force is completely achieved. That technique also facilitates to master such a method as "Strength of Eagle's Claws" YING ZHAO LI FA (see par.#35), because success will be also achieved in training the "soft" YIN force. The exercise being acquired, it will be of no importance if an enemy or some thing is in front of you: the only thing you have to do is to raise your arm and the enemy or the thing will be also risen. That method can not cause death but it can injure muscles and bones, it has resemblance in that to the method "Strength of Eagle's Claws".

68. Claws of Mantis
(TANGLANG ZHAO)

*This hard and tenacious work must
be done constantly and diligently.*

"Claws of Mantis" is "hard" exercise which strengthens the
"external". It develops the "hard" YANG force but also
contains "soft" YIN force. That exercise is also called
"Diamond Hand" – JINGANG SHOU. It strengthens,
through training, the edge of a palm and a wrist. In outward
appearance it resembles training in "force ejection" ("force
outburst") of the exercise "Palm of Guan Yin"[129], but its
essence is completely different. Here the force of the forearm
moving from above downward is used and it is completely
"hard force". It is one of combat arms techniques employed at
the shortest distance and here life or death of the enemy
depends upon the bent wrist. The effect from a blow is a sort
of chopping with an axe and movements resemble a mantis
which defends itself, hence, the name – "Claws of Mantis".
Similar chops can be often found among techniques of QUAN
FA[130]. But the difference of the Shaolin school is that arm
chops in this case are partly executed with employment of

Editor's notes:

[129] see par.#70.
[130] QUAN FA, lit. "Fist Techniques".

"soft" force where "softness" conceals "hardness" and it is the most efficient employment of this technique.

To do that exercise, it is necessary to make a pile of ten bricks, put above a sheaf of paper about 3 CUNs (10 cm) thick. Stand nearby, draw out a forearm and press the shoulder close to ribs, concentrate all the force in the wrist. The distance from the hand to the paper is about 3 CUNs (10 cm), the thumb is pointed up, the outer edge of the palm faces down. When doing the exercise, it is necessary at first to bend with force the wrist so that fingers be pointed upward and the outer edge of the palm, that is on the side of the little finger, forward. Then make a downward chopping movement with a strike at the pile of bricks covered with a paper layer with the edge of the palm. Do the technique with both hands in turn, or first with one hand then with the other. Exercise two times every day, deliver a hundred or more blows during a training session, with a gradual increase of the number of blows. Increase gradually to 500 blows with each hand during a training session. At first no effect is evident, but one year later the bricks under a paper layer will start to break into several pieces under palm blows, finally the whole pile of bricks will be completely broken. After it put one more sheaf of paper, 3 CUNs thick, remove one or two bricks from the pile and continue training as before, trying to break all bricks. Then remove one or two bricks again and add a sheaf of paper etc. Over time the thickness of paper pile will reach two CHIs (66 cm) with only one brick under it and that brick must be broken by a palm blow. With that the mastery in the employment of "hard" force (SI JIN) is completely formed.

Now it is necessary to change the method of doing exercise and practice in "live (or lively) force" HUO JIN. It is very difficult to match and unite "hard force" with "lively force" in reality. At first, train yourself as follows: take one tile, put it vertically on the ground, prop up with bricks from sides to keep it in the position. Then strike (horizontally) with the edge of a palm. The tile will fall without splitting at the beginning. It is necessary to exercise until you learn to break the tile, pieces of the tile will have to fall on the ground. It is necessary, then, to learn "cutting" the upper part of tile so that the lower part propped up by bricks may remain to stand vertically. When you succeed in splitting the tile without its fall on the ground, propping-up bricks should be removed. It is necessary to stick the tile slightly into the ground to keep it in the vertical position and strike at it. Again, it will be necessary to succeed in "cutting" the upper part of tile with a palm, the lower part should not fall, even not sway. With that the exercise has 70% efficiency.

Now take a thickest brick and train yourself as before, trying to get capability of splitting the thickest bricks used for building town walls. Then replace the brick with a stone. If your palm cuts a piece from the stone and the stone itself does not overturn, the exercise "Claws of Mantis" approaches its final stage, but for that it is necessary to learn to transform "hardness" into "softness". One has to spend a lot of time for that exercise, 7 or 8 years at least. If a man is a slow-witted from nature, even 10 years will not be enough to master that exercise.

After successful acquirement of that exercise it is necessary for a wrist and a palm to be filled with force when you encounter an enemy, in that case there will be no man who will be invincible for you. In usual peaceful situation it is no need to use force, so your palm will not differ from a palm of an ordinary man. If you touch (unintentionally) the body of some man, you will not inflict a wound on him. The efficiency of that skill is comparable with the splendid skill of "Deadly YIN Hand" – YIN SHOU SHA REN. At the beginning, it is necessary to use a pile of paper to develop the "soft force". The "soft force" goes through the paper that separates bricks from your hand, then it transforms into the "hard force". "Hardness" and "softness" supplement each other skillfully and naturally.

At first that exercise got to Shaolin, from there it spread along the right bank of Yangtze to its whole length and later in other places to become very popular with contemporaries. There are also such techniques as "13 Mantis Claw Techniques" and a complete Mantis style with a great number of techniques and methods. They are of independent significance, but they do not belong to this GONG FU.

69. Skill "Bag" (BU DAI GONG)

The exercise "Bag" is the "soft" Gong Fu, it develops "internal" power and belongs to the YIN category, but it contains some elements of YANG. It is not training with a bag, that is the name of a method for exercising the stomach. The training purport is the development of ability to withstand enemies attacks.

At the first stage of the training process it is necessary to sit, calm down thoughts and breath, strain QI in the region of the waist[131]. Stroke the stomach with both hands 36 times: the left hand moves first, then the right one. Release QI[132], then stroke with both hands in the reverse direction[133]. Repeat several times in that manner. In one or two years your stomach will become as soft as silk. However, if you strain QI, your stomach becomes as hard as iron. After that stand a support and lay a log on it. Press your stomach to its butt-end, strain QI, try to embrace the butt-end with your stomach and pull the log back. At the beginning the log will surely fall out. But over time, after long

---

Editor's notes:

[131] Most probably, it implies so-called "belly breathing" when the chest is immovable and breathing movements are done due to straining and relaxing muscles of the stomach, especially muscles of its lower part.
[132] The term QI is known to have several meanings, in particular, "internal energy" and "air". So, most probably, "release QI" in this context means a deep breath-out and mental relaxation.
[133] Here circular motions of hands are evidently implied.

training, you will learn to "drawn in" the log so it cannot be pulled off even with great effort. It means full success has been gained. Now if you "drawn in" the butt-end of the log with your stomach and then strain QI and abruptly push out the log, it will fly directly forward. If the enemy punches at your stomach, his fist will stick in the stomach and it will be difficult to pull the fist out – such a feeling as if handcuffs were locked, causing pain. Even spears and swords can do no harm. BU DAI GONG is a combination of YIN and YANG with "hardness" and "softness" to supplement each other. This kind of GONG FU is not to be identified with the "hard" GONG FU "Iron Bull" (see par.#36), they are different methods.

It needs 10 years of hard work to get full success. I had occasions to see Shang Yung Siang's performances when he withstood the strongest blows at his stomach and "drawn in" an attacking fist – they were wonderful shows.

70. Palm of Guan Yin (GUAN YIN ZHANG)

The exercise "Palm of Guan Yin" has another name "Sword for the Extermination of Evil Spirits". It is the "soft" Gong Fu which develops "outer" power, it belongs to the YIN category. It is a method of exercising a wrist and a palm for effective using the technique of "chopping hand" in hand-to-hand fight.

At first training is as follows: it is necessary to strike at a tree with the edge of a palm. You have to train yourself to the degree when a clear mark is left after each of your blows at a tree. After that the tree can be replaced with a stone. After one or two years of such training a blow at a stone will break off small pieces from it. But it is not success yet. When a stone is split by a blow and a cut is a sort of knife cutting, use a pan with iron shot instead of a stone. The thickness of a shot layer must be a little bit more than one CHI (33 cm). Exercise in striking as before. At first a striking palm simply immerses into shot, but when you take away your palm, shot returns to its place. But after long training you will learn to strike such a blow that shot will fly away from the palm and will not gather[134]. However, you have to continue training and reach the state when shot would fly away at a distance not more than one CUN (3.3 cm) and no

---

Editor's notes:

[134] That is, a pit appears at the spot where a strike was made.

pellet is left on the bottom of the pan[135]. If in that case you strike several successive blows at different places, shot can be divided into few groups that will look like soy-bean pudding cut with a knife evenly and exactly. With that comes the perfect mastery in GUAN YIN ZHANG. As the palm becomes like a knife, it is advised to exercise the left hand to avoid unintentional infliction of body damages.

Editor's notes:

[135] It implies the bottom of the pan at the spot where a strike was made, i.e. your palm must reach the bottom of the pan.

71. Skill "Raising a Pot" (SHANG GUAN GONG)

SHANG GUAN GONG is the "hard" Gong Fu, it develops "external" power and belongs to the YANG category. The purport of this exercise is strengthening shoulders and the grip of both hands.

It is done in such a manner: take a small pot with two eyelets and tie up a short cord to them. Take another cord 3 or 4 CHIs long (1 m – 1.30 m) and tie one of its ends to the middle part of the short cord and the other end to a short stick. The stick must be about 1.2 CHI (about 40 cm), its diameter should be appropriate for a convenient holding. It is desirable that the stick should be of date-palm and with rough surface.

Bore a hole at the middle of the stick, put the free end of the long cord through that hole and make a knot. The weight of an empty pot is about 3 – 3.5 kg. Fill it with 1.5 kg of iron shot – at the initial stage the total weight should not be more than 5 kg.

Take the stance "Rider" (MA BU) during a training session, the upper part of the body being erect, hold the stick with both hands and raise the pot. Your elbows should be at the level of the shoulders, the forearms directed forward and a little upward. Rotate the stick to yourself with both hands in turn to wind up the cord. Raise the pot to the chest level, then after a small pause slowly lower the pot. Do it 30 times. Exercise in such a manner each morning and evening. After three months add half a kilogram of shot. Continue to add 0.5 kg of shot in each three months, five times all in all. Thus, the weight of the pot will increase by 2.5 kg. After that continue adding shot once during three months to increase the weight of the pot to 15 kg. By that time the trainee has great strength. If you stand on rising ground, which will permit to have a longer cord - up to 5 CHIs (1.65 cm), the result will be still better. On the North a lot of people exercise this kind of Gong Fu. It needs at least 3 years to get success. At my time I also practiced (this kind of Gong Fu), but due to some circumstances I could not carry that matter through and I am very sorry about it.

72. Rubbing Palms (HE PAN ZHANG)

If somebody practices in squeezing various things with force, it is a good method to learn to twist even the hardest things. Later, even an iron chopstick can be knotted and pressed so that it will become very thin and its length will increase as much as twice. It is only doubtful if that chopstick will be still suitable for application.

The technique "Rubbing[136] Palms", sometimes called "Hand of Golden Dragon", is the most effective among all known methods of the pugilistic art which are anyhow connected to "rubbing" movements. Training in this technique is also aimed at strengthening outer power of the body and rearing the YANG force in it.

The method of acquiring the technique "Rubbing Palms" is very and very simple. Take 30 bamboo chopsticks, best of all, square ones. Gather the sticks in one bundle and tie it up with a thin thread in several places. It is necessary to tie the sticks so that

---

Editor's notes:

[136]"Twisting", "wrenching", "pressing" etc. in this text imply the same movement, that is: palms are put together (as in a prayer) with a thing (a bunch of chopsticks) pressed between them, palms move back and forth in respect to each other, it is the movement when one rubs palms.

not to leave even a millimeter of space between them. The sticks must be pressed to each other so tightly that they may not move. Surely, it will be difficult for you at first to tie chopsticks so. If there is space left between them, keep inserting more sticks there until your bunch has the proper view.

Then you have to take the chopsticks with both hands, press them between the palms and rub the bunch to roll on each of your palms. It should be done with force. The left palm must also move in respect to the right one and turn the bunch with force. When you are exhausted, take a little rest. Then squeeze the bunch of sticks again in your palms and rub it with all your strength between the palms. This exercise should be done several times each day.

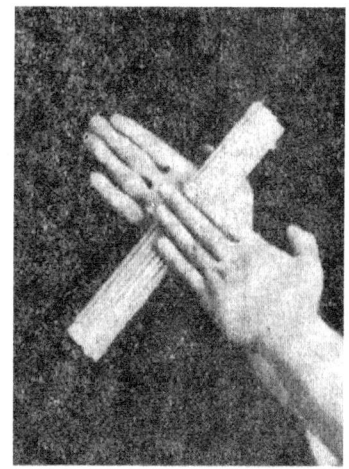

Over time chopsticks will be pressed in a bunch ever tighter. At last, they will be so close to each other, that even a silk thread can not be thrust through them. After two years when you make a little progress in learning HE PAN ZHANG, the outer sticks if twisted will start to break and intertwine and the inner sticks to turn over, though the bunch is tightly fixed with threads. Now you may proceed to training with metal chopsticks.

The training method with metal chopsticks does not differ from that one with bamboo sticks. After two years when metal thumb-thick sticks are thinned to a thickness of small fingers and the length of the sticks increases as much as twice or more, it will mean that you have made every effort "during 1000 days" and it will be seen by naked eye. At that moment it will become clear that you have fully mastered the skill. It is beyond any doubts now that you will be able to cope with any thing just by stretching an arm and touching it. You will be able to break something instantly, crumple any iron or stone thing. Nothing can resist you strongly, not to mention men of flesh and blood.

A great wizard from Jiangnan, the inventor of this exercise, described it in his book. He related that when somebody acquires this method, wood will seem to him as soft as vegetables. You will be able to break a bamboo into small pieces, fray a steel rope with your fingers. The only thing you need to do is to stretch your arm and touch a gate, and the most strongest bolts will be opened. There is still a vast number of methods of application of that skill. Surely, that technique can be effectively used for repelling an enemy's attack.

They say even a steel pole can be ground off into a needle with a profound mastery in stock.

***

Shaolin Kung Fu Online Library
www.kungfulibrary.com

Chinese Martial Arts - Theory & Practice
Old Chinese Books, Treatises, Manuscripts

Lam Sai Wing. Moving Along the Hieroglyph Gung, I Tame the Tiger with the Pugilistic Art.

Lam Sai Wing. Tiger and Crane Double Form.

Lam Sai Wing. TIET SIN: Iron Thread.

Jin Jing Zhong. Training Methods of 72 Arts of Shaolin.

Jin Jing Zhong. Dian Xue Shu: Skill of Acting on Acupoints.

Liu Jin Sheng. CHIN NA FA: Skill of Catch and Hold.

Tang Ji Ren. Pugilistic Art of the Tang Family. DA HONG QUAN.

Xu Yi Qian. CHUAN NA QUAN: Style of Piercing Blows and Holds.

Yuan Chu Cai. MEI HUA ZHUANG: Poles of Plum Blossom. External and Internal Training.